INSIDE OUT
WHEN GRIEF BECOMES A GIFT

KIM CAMERON

Praise for Inside Out

On first read of Kim's memoir *Inside Out*, I cried—for Kim, for Ella, their family and friends, and to my surprise, for my own grief. Thank you, Kim, for having the courage to write from your heart about the unthinkable in your gentle, beautiful way that allows my own grief to heal a little and leaves me with a sense of hope.

Karen Collyer, Author *Hermione's Hope*,
Psychosomatic Therapist and Intuitive Communicator

Kim Cameron's honest sharing of the devastating loss of her daughter, Ella, is heart-rending and compelling. Grief is a deeply personal yet completely universal experience; talking about it is healing for all of us. Kim invites the reader to feel and to heal as she shares some of the reflections and processes that helped her put herself back together – from the inside out – after one of the most shattering losses imaginable. I honour her commitment to her own healing and her profound desire to be of service to others.

Dawn Albinger, 'Spirit of Woman' Retreat Facilitator

Inside Out
When Grief Becomes a Gift

Kim Cameron

© 2023 Kim Cameron. All rights reserved.
Published in 2023 by Kim Cameron.

All rights reserved. No part of this document may be reproduced or transmitted in any form or by any means, electronic, mechanical, photocopying, recording or otherwise, or by any information storage and retrieval system, without prior written permission of Kim Cameron or publisher (except by a reviewer, who may quote brief passages and/or show brief video clips in a review).

For permissions and orders:
Kim Cameron email: kimleannecameron@gmail.com
https://www.kimcameronholistictherapies.com.au

Prepublication Data Service Details available from: the National Library of Australia
ISBN 978-0-6458779-1-5 (paperback)
ISBN 978-0-6458779-2-2 (eBook)

Disclaimer
This book, a memoir, depicts actual events in the life of the author as truthfully as her memory allows. Dialogue of each person speaking has been written as accurately as the author was able to recollect, with the goal of keeping true to the character of all persons mentioned. While all persons mentioned are actual people, some names have been changed to respect the privacy of the persons concerned.

To my darling Ella, Timothy and Sam.
Thank you for choosing me to be your mum.

Inside Out

When Grief Becomes a Gift

**One woman's commitment to herself to
heal from the Inside Out.**

How do you re-enter life after the sudden death of your only daughter?

Kim tells of her personal journey, looking deep within her own soul as she commits to living a life of purpose in honor of her little girl, Ella, who passed away suddenly at the age of ten from a rare brain malformation her family had no idea she had.

Through extensive Retreat Work as a participant and facilitator, together with a wide range of alternative therapies (including Holistic Counselling, Kinesiology, Art and Sand Therapy, Meditation, Cathartic Breathwork and KaHuna Bodywork) Kim experienced profound and life-changing moments that changed the way she sees herself and the world around her.

Becoming a practitioner as part of her journey, Kim found her purpose and passion in providing safe spaces for others to be supported in their own healing. Being witness to her own transformation and sitting with many others committed to do the same as they step into the most vulnerable places within, processing layers of suppressed emotions and creating space for deeper connection, is one of the greatest gifts Kim has received in her life.

This gift came to her through her own experience of deep grief.

A Message from Kim

**Being courageous doesn't mean you aren't afraid.
Being courageous means you draw on your inner strength to embrace being afraid and still move forward.**

This book is written from my heart, with the intention that it may provide hope if you have experienced loss, trauma, grief, or are struggling with life in any way.

Life throws us all a unique combination of experiences and challenges to navigate through to enable our own personal growth, and this will continue.

Setting out on your own path with curiosity towards yourself, your emotions, feelings, and your surroundings can be exciting and daunting at the same time. When I see you on your own journey with an open heart and mind, my own heart feels love and deep compassion for you. I know the journey well—wandering the planet searching for what lies deep within your soul, often not realising you already have everything you need inside, just waiting for you to stop long enough to process, let go, connect and surrender as you witness your own evolution.

Never give up hope. Along this journey, amongst the heartache, pain and challenges, you will often find yourself in places you feel you do not want to be, yet it is in those places you'll find exactly what you're looking for—you!

At the end of this book I have included journal prompts and reflections for you as an invitation, should you wish to dive a little deeper within yourself. You will also find a link there to download the Inside Out Reflection and Connection Journal, should you wish to use this.

You'll see that each chapter has its own reflection song. Music has played a big part in my life. I hope you feel its connective power through the songs I've chosen to share (there is a QR Code to the Spotify playlist in the back of the book or you can search for each song online).

Give yourself time and space as you read. Stop if you need to, to reflect on your own life and the emotions and feelings that may arise as you move through each chapter.

If you're experiencing grief and find big tasks overwhelming, I hope you'll feel encouraged by the short chapters, just enough to inspire you on the days that concentrating for long periods of time might be challenging.

I understand parts of this book might be triggering for some and bring up deep emotions. Be kind to yourself. Know that this is all ok and exactly how it is meant to be unfolding for you. Most emotions that surface have been ignored and pushed down in our bodies for way too long, just waiting for the opportunity and space to be acknowledged and felt. I recommend you seek support if you feel this would be beneficial for you (contact details for some support organisations are at the back of the book).

My story is my personal, individual journey that I moved through with an open heart and mind, with love, determination, and often fear, to ensure my life was one of purpose and compassion. At times, I had no idea what to expect as I entered spaces that were unknown and unfamiliar to me. One thing I always knew deep within was that change was always on the other side of fear!

I was the lucky one—gifted the opportunity to live on this planet longer than my daughter—and I was determined to do this with conscious awareness, to become the best possible version of myself, learning each step of the way.

Living life to the fullest, every day I am given the gift of opening my eyes once more—for myself, for my beautiful Ella, for my precious sons, Sam and Timothy, and for my devoted husband, Robert. Every day, it is a choice I make.

If through this process I am able to create space and inspire others to do the same, then I feel my purpose on this planet will be fulfilled.

If you have this book in your hands, it is with you for a reason. Take what you need from it and leave the rest.

I hope you see *Inside Out* as a gift and an opportunity to look within your own beautiful heart and soul with gentleness, grace, love and acceptance.

With Eternal Love and Gratitude
Kim
x

I Was

I was a mum of three,
Then one day I was no more.
My life revolved around you,
Coming in and out that door.

We did everything together,
Thought we had endless time.
Little did we know,
There was a mountain we had to climb.

Never in my worst nightmare,
Did I think you would not be,
Right beside my bed,
Asking for cuddles at half past three.

And at the time I thought,
You really should be back in bed.
Oh god in heaven, what I would give,
To have your little face lie near my head.

You never think you'll be the one,
Whose child dies before you do.
It's just not the way it's meant to be,
I thought it happened to so few.

You don't want to be that person,
You don't want to walk through those doors.
But when you're given no other choice,
You have to accept this life is now yours.

God took your child, way too soon,
For reasons you'll never know.
So much anger, grief and sadness,
Where to start? Where to go?

They say that time will heal.
Well, how exactly do they know?
Unless they've walked in my shoes,
Time is endless, time is slow.

So each day I try to remember,
Your laughter and your smile,
The gift of love you gave to us,
Even if only for a little while.

Ten short years seemed like nothing,
When we thought time was on our side.
So many questions with no answers,
The oceans I have cried.

We have so many memories,
That we talk about all the time.
It's so hard not to see you,
But in my heart, I know you're fine.

I know you're always with me,
I feel you late at night.
But I miss you so much, baby girl,
This pain just isn't right.

Sometimes people look at me,
And I wonder what they think.
I am not the person that I was,
I can't repair the missing link.

Inside I feel so broken,
No matter how hard I try to hide.
The pain of losing a child,
Feels impossible to heal inside.

So each day I wake and remember,
That my life is not the same.
But I think of you, my baby girl,
As I stare at your photo in that frame.

I think of all you taught me,
And what you'd say to me right now,
And I get out of my bed once more,
And I try to make you proud.

But really all I'm doing,
Is pushing me aside.
Because as soon as I slow down again,
It eats away inside.

The reality won't go away,
I feel I am no longer me.
I'm still a mum, a wife, a friend,
Just not the same inside, you see.

Please don't try to fix me,
It's impossible to do.
My life has changed and so have I,
I'm not the same person that you knew.

So when you look at me,
And wonder who I have become,
I'm still a mum, a wife, a friend,
I'll always be Ella's mum…
Kim Cameron

Contents

Part 1
1. The 7th of June 1
2. Keep Her Safe 4
3. Anniversary 12
4. Labour Day 16
5. The Circle of Life 22
6. Ella's Parents 27
7. The Front Door 36
8. Goodbye 40
9. Treading Water 48

Part 2
10. Vilomah 57
11. Just Do It 60
12. What Are You Going To Do Now? 64
13. My Boys 71
14. Grief 76
15. New Beginnings for Some 82
16. My First Retreat 86
17. Processing in Circles 90
18. Ella's Walk 99
19. I'm Scared 105
20. It's Time 109
21. Spirit of Woman 115
22. KaHuna Homecoming 121
23. How Do We Connect Again? 127
24. Listen Carefully 131
25. Moving Forward 138
26. Taking the Plunge 144
27. Leave Your Negativity and Your Shoes
    at the Door 151

28. I Am Back 155
29. Shake It Up 162
30. Integration 171
31. Friendships 177
32. Mother's Day 180
33. The Time has Come 184
34. The Show Must Go On 190
35. Reconnection Retreat 196
36. What Do You Love? 206
37. Conversations 210
38. Rites of Passage 214
39. Heartbeats 219
40. Marathon 223
41. The Morning After 227
42. Re-entry Into the World 233
43. Full Moon 238
44. Five Minutes More 243
45. December 248
46. Home Retreat 254
47. Time Off 262
48. Reflecting in Nature 264
49. Within the Busyness 267
50. Another Year 271
51. Preparation 275
52. Surprise! 280
53 The Next Part of the Journey 283

Important Things I've Learnt on This Journey 287
An Invitation for Reflection and Deeper Connection 291
Song List 303
Poems by Kim Cameron 306
Organisations for Support in Australia 307
About the Author 309

Part 1

1
The 7ᵗʰ of June

*'In the blink of an eye, everything can change.
So, forgive often and love with all your heart.
You may never know when you may not have
that chance again.'*
                                                    Zig Ziglar

June 7, 2014

'I need you to sign these papers—if we don't operate on your daughter immediately, she will die.'

As I'm being told this, my little girl is wheeled swiftly past me on a hospital bed, her young body lifeless and unconscious. I am in a different, unfamiliar world.

I look to the doctor, 'You need to let me know what the best possible outcome of this is going to be.'

In my gut, I already know the worst, but I don't want to think about or hear any of that. All I can do is focus on whatever piece of positive information he can give me right now.

'Your daughter will not be able to speak, walk, or do most of the things she used to. Her symptoms will be like that of a stroke patient. Her brain is bleeding and has already sustained severe damage.'

This is the best news he can give me.

I sign the papers in an attempt to save her life.

Part 1 – The 7th of June

We could cope with that, if she were coming home with us, we could cope with that. I keep telling myself this over and over.

≈

'You need to get her dad so he can see her before she goes into theatre,' I tell the nurse. She looks to the doctor—there's no time; however, the beautiful nurse who has been with me from the moment I ran into the Emergency Department of the John Hunter Hospital has already gone. She was beside me as I faced the devastating vision of my ten-year-old daughter lying unconscious, surrounded by doctors, nurses and a crash cart—ready to be intubated. She found him, waiting in the family room with my husband, Rob.

Ella's dad arrives just as I finish signing the papers. We're rushed into the operating theatre where Ella lies unconscious, in an induced coma. Doctors and nurses busily prepare for the procedure to stop the massive bleed taking place in her little brain.

I look at her fragile body. Kissing her face, I tell her I love her and that she is going to be ok.

There's no time for anything else. They need us out of here.

They need to save our daughter's life.

The huge bright light shining down from above her haunts me for some reason. That, and the hectic pace of everyone moving so quickly, makes it feel like I'm watching a scene from outside of my own body. As we are quickly ushered out of the operating theatre and through the large swinging doors, I turn to look at my baby girl one last time. The shock hits me like a wrecking ball.

My legs start to tingle and feel weak. I double over, with the sickest feeling in my stomach. My heart races and my head spins. I lower myself to the floor before I fall as the intensity of what's happening physically takes over my body. Until now, I've been running on adrenaline, trying to keep it together, trying not to panic, while every cell in my body feels like they're being turned inside out.

How could this be happening?

My whole world feels out of control. The fear is like nothing I've ever experienced. I've just left my little girl's life in the hands of people I don't even know! There was no other choice. The realisation of what is happening is overwhelming.

I force myself to breathe deeply and receive some comfort from Craig (Ella's dad) and the nurse who is still with us. Drawing on all the strength I have, I slowly stand up. I must keep it together somehow and stay as positive as I can. If I fall apart, especially in front of my boys, they'll know how bad this situation is and how terrified I am. This will only instill more fear in them, and that's not what I want to do. I have always been their safe place to land. I don't know how to be that in this moment. I do my best to stay in control of myself, while inside, my heart is breaking and my body is screaming.

Walking back through the Emergency Department, we're led into the Family Room. There sits Rob, my boys (Sam and Tim) and Craig's wife. They'd all arrived while this traumatic cluster of events was taking place on the other side of the wall. Although they know things are not good, they have no idea just how bad things are.

To be honest—neither do I.

Reflection Song: Hand to Hold—JJ Heller

2

Keep Her Safe

*'Hope is important because it can make the
present moment less difficult to bear.'*
Thich Nhat Hanh

A few hours earlier, I'd received a phone call.

Ella and her brothers were spending the weekend at their dad's house, as they did every fortnight. It was the long weekend in June, normally a weekend we'd all have gone away in different directions, but for some reason none of us had. Rob and I were sitting down having dinner when the phone rang.

I answered to Craig's voice—telling me there was something wrong with Ella. My first thoughts were that maybe she'd broken her arm or leg jumping on the trampoline or hurt herself doing some crazy dance move or cartwheel, like the ones she'd asked me to watch her do in our front yard the day before.

How I wish that was all it was—a broken bone that could mend.

He continued, telling me Ella had complained of a sudden headache and collapsed. She is now unconscious and unresponsive, in a speeding ambulance on her way to the best hospital in our area, as our local hospital is not equipped to deal with what's happening.

≈

My heart races and my stomach churns as anxiety and fear take over my mind and body.

'I'm on my way.'

Rob and I race to the hospital—the longest half-hour drive of my life! My body rocks back and forth on the inside as I unconsciously try to soothe myself, praying over and over again that she will be ok. This is not something I've made a conscious decision to do—it just happens. I'm on autopilot.

Please keep her safe. Please keep her safe. This thought plays in my head on a constant, repetitive loop.

Not knowing the severity of what is actually happening, I try not to suspect the worst, yet know from what I've already been told that this is not a good situation.

Thoughts of my aunty flood my mind. A few years earlier, she was rushed to the same hospital with a severe headache caused by an aneurysm, resulting in us having to make the heartbreaking decision to turn off her life support after weeks of brain surgery and complications. I try to tell myself this is not the same; however, it's the closest thing I've experienced to what I'm hearing—and it's happening to my daughter!

I have no idea what is really going on in her little body. I need to be with her.

Sudden headache. Unconscious. Not a good combination.

Rob drops me at the hospital's front entrance and goes to park the car. I run into the Emergency Department, straight to the counter.

'I'm Ella's mum.'

The doors immediately open and I'm led to a curtained-off room. I see Craig standing back, watching in disbelief, a look of utter helplessness across his face.

I look into his eyes and ask, 'What the hell is going on?'

Part 1 – Keep Her Safe

As his eyes fill with tears, he tells one of the doctors I'm Ella's mum. They start to explain what is happening. I'm not sure I am comprehending what they're saying—my eyes are fixated on my baby girl. She's not moving. Tubes and cannulas are coming out of her body. They tell me they're about to intubate her and put her in an induced coma so she won't remember anything.

I kiss her little face and tell her, 'Mummy is here now, baby girl. Everything is going to be ok.'

Everything is going to be ok? A promise I could never keep. What else can I say? Maybe she can still hear me. I hold her small hand and look at the floor until the procedure is over. Tears roll down my cheeks.

Ella is now in an induced coma. I have to stand back and let the doctors do their job. Standing next to Craig, we watch helplessly. How can this be happening to our beautiful little girl?

As they work to stabilise Ella enough to get her to the x-ray department for an urgent brain scan, I tell them I'm going with her. I will not leave her side. The nurse asks the doctor and thank God, he lets me. Although I know there's nothing I can do, I cannot let her out of my sight. She is rushed into x-ray, surrounded by doctors and nurses. Someone wheels a crash cart next to her.

Ella is placed ever so gently onto the MRI machine. Her fragile body is moved in and out as her brain is scanned. I stand inside the room where they view her images on the screen. They start to talk, and the nurse reminds them I am present. I don't hear exactly what is said, but I know from the urgency I am surrounded by that it's not good. The nursing staff go to move Ella back onto the hospital bed and are reprimanded by their head nurse, who instructs them not to move her in any way until she says so. This is serious. Very serious.

The beautiful nurse who has been with me the whole time starts asking me about Ella. I guess she's trying to distract me from the trauma unfolding in front of my eyes. I tell her what a beautiful, determined girl she is and how much she loves dancing. I talk about how funny she is and how she gives her big brothers a hard time, while learning some really 'interesting' things from both of them, including posting selfies together on Instagram and learning all the high school jargon and lingo (an added bonus when you're the youngest of three). I guess this will prepare her for high school in less than two years' time. We talk for a couple of minutes while I watch Ella out of the corner of my eye, never letting her out of my sight.

Now it's time to move—quickly, into the operating theatre. This is a critical, life-threatening situation, and everyone knows it.

Ella's life is now in the hands of the surgeons.

Back in the Family Room, Rob knows by the way I look at him that everything is not ok. I don't need to say anything. He puts his arm around me as tears trickle down my cheeks. I can see he's been crying.

I try to hold it together as best I can, at least on the outside.

I feel so sick.

My boys, just sixteen and nineteen, don't really know the full extent of what's going on. I look at them and my heart breaks. They shouldn't have to experience this. None of us should. Knowing I can't protect them, I try to explain what is happening—that Ella has had a massive brain bleed and doctors are now operating on her brain to try and stop it.

The nurse told me this can be a relatively simple operation once the bleed has been located and stopped and may only take around an hour or so. However, I know the bleeding that has already taken place has caused significant brain damage. I try to remain hopeful, as that is all I have—hope!

We are taken upstairs to the Intensive Care Unit waiting room. Nobody knows what to say. I go over and over with Craig to get as many details as I can as to exactly what happened so I can get it clear in my mind and try to understand how this is even possible.

Ella was calm and happy when her headache occurred, quickly taking over her body. She was practicing a laidback dance routine in the lounge room, as she regularly did. She wasn't cartwheeling around the backyard or standing on her head doing the splits like she loved to do. She wasn't running around crazy. She was just being a regular ten-year-old little girl doing what she loved most—dance.

What had my poor baby gone through in those moments? I hate to think of the pain and fear that moved through her as she screamed for her dad to help her, before collapsing, her helpless body in shock, slowly shutting down in order to survive.

I start to pray again—*please keep Ella safe, please keep Ella safe, please keep Ella safe*—it's like a mantra in my head. I'm not sure where this comes from, as I'm not someone who prays regularly. It's an intuitive response, yet out of desperation at the same time.

I sit. I stand. I pace, for what feels like hours, waiting.

I call my sister, Kylie. I don't want to put any stress on her as she's eighteen weeks pregnant, but I need to talk to her, and I know she would want me to call. I try to tell her as calmly as I can what is happening. I break down. I am so bloody scared right now, and I know no one can take away this fear.

Kylie is on her way to be with me. She's my only sibling and loves me and my children dearly.

Time ticks by. An hour passes.

I start pacing the hallway again.

Why is it taking so long?

I know I must be patient and let them do their job, but I just want to know what is happening. It is torturous.

Kylie is here. She's holding me in her arms. My heart is broken open and a flood of emotions I've been holding in is rushing out.

I let it go, just for a minute.

Now I pull myself together.

This is not a time for me to fall apart. I need to be strong. I need to be strong for Ella, for my boys and for Rob.

I just need to be strong and try to stay positive.

I know that when my fear fully takes over it's going to be hard for me to come back from that. *Keep thinking of the best possible outcome,* I tell myself. This is not what we had imagined our daughter's life to be like when we brought her into this world, but if it means we get to take her home, we will all adjust and manage to give her the best life possible.

I can't think any further ahead than right now. Actually, I really can't think at all.

In the blink of an eye, our whole world has changed—is changing—in each second as we wait, and I have no control over any of it. This is the most frightening moment of my life.

I've been waiting to call my parents. I was hoping to call them once I knew exactly what was happening and not put them through any unnecessary worry, but as time goes on,

Part 1 – Keep Her Safe

I feel the need to call them becoming stronger. The surgery is taking longer than I'd expected and each minute feels like an hour.

This is a call I really don't want to make.

My mum has already been through the trauma of her younger sister having emergency brain surgery, and here we are again—same hospital, same waiting room where we spent so many hours before—waiting.

Waiting.

This is not right. How can this be happening again to our family?

How can this be happening to my only daughter?

She's just a child.

She's, my baby.

In this moment, I wish I could take her place.

I wish it was me.

I don't want her to have to be experiencing any of this.

I don't want to have to be experiencing any of this.

It feels like I am being tortured.

My heart is in so much pain.

I take a few deep breaths and call.

No answer.

I call again.

No answer.

I call their mobile phones.

No answer.

I'm starting to feel desperate. *Please! I just want someone to pick up the bloody phone!*

I want to talk to my dad. I feel like I can't talk to Mum right now.

I don't want to have to be the one to tell her what is happening. I know I cannot cope with her shock and panic right now, which is inevitable and a normal reaction to her hearing what is happening to her granddaughter. It's just too much for me to feel and I can't risk taking on anyone else's emotions while I try to calm myself internally in any way possible.

I feel like I am in a state of survival, just trying so hard not to fall apart.

I know the surgeon could walk out of those doors at any minute and I need to be able to stay calm and be able to comprehend everything he has to tell me.

I start to chant in my head—*Dad, please pick up the phone, please pick up the phone.*

For God's sake! Someone pick up the god damn phone!

It's around 9.30 on Saturday night. I assume they're already in bed and cannot even hear the phone.

I try once more, and Dad finally answers. Thank God!

I feel relieved, but the reality of what I have to tell him hits me. I can't get the words out. How do you put it into words?

My dad (Pa) and Ella have an incredibly beautiful bond. She pretty much worships the ground he walks on, and he her. They spend time doing the fun stuff all girls love to do—like going fishing, working in the garage hammering nails into pieces of wood, gardening and creating things out of junk. Ella even has her own pink hammer and toolbox at Pa and Nan's house.

I try to explain what is happening and that I think they should get to the hospital as soon as possible. I leave it with him to tell Mum. Talking to Mum will just unravel so much more emotion in me and I'm not sure I can cope with that.

Reflection Song: A Mother's Prayer—Céline Dion

3

Anniversary

'The trouble is you think you have time.'
Buddha

We're surrounded by family now from all sides, all waiting patiently for any sort of news.

I can't wait any longer—it's been hours. I pick up the phone outside the operating theatre that connects to the inside and hope someone answers. They do. I tell them I'm Ella's mum and I want to know if they can tell me anything at all about what is happening with my daughter.

I want them to tell me she is in recovery, and everything went well.

But they don't.

They tell me she is still in theatre, and they are still working on her.

My heart sinks. Anxiety becomes stronger as the lump in my throat feels like it is blocking my airway.

I know in my heart they are doing everything they can to stop the bleed that is flooding Ella's little brain, but why is it taking so long?

I justify to myself that brain surgery is complicated. I tell myself stories in my head about why it is taking longer than they expected, trying to keep my sanity intact with my own positive self-talk.

I pray some more.

And we wait.

I haven't been inside a church for many years, but in desperation, part of me feels called to go to the chapel downstairs and beg God to save my little girl. But I know I can't leave the space I am in, in case we get any news. So, I stay and continue to pray, silently.

I pray her strength and determination will get her through what she is enduring. I know she is strong. *Come on, chicken* (as we like to call her), *you can do this. Stay strong, baby girl.*

She is such a beautiful soul. I think about all the things she loves—being outdoors, going camping and to the beach. Spending hours in the water is where she is in her element, especially being taken out beyond her depth to ride the waves. She loves horse riding and is an animal lover. Her new puppy, Jessie, a Puggle we picked up only four weeks ago, is waiting at home for her. Dance brings her so much joy. Most of all, she loves being with her family. She loves to just lounge around at home, and if she has someone sitting beside her that she can lie all over, even better. She has a lot of sass and can be very stubborn (like her mum). I love everything about her.

My parents arrive. It's hard to see them here, having to experience all of this with us, but in my heart, I know we all need to be here together. I can't protect them from reality, and it is not my job to do so.

I break down when I see them. They hold me.

I sit with my mum and drink a cup of peppermint tea someone has made me. I try to focus on the warm feeling that surrounds my hands, but it's hard to feel any warmth.

I turn to her and say, 'This is not good, Mum.' She knows. She doesn't try to protect me, but looks at me and says, 'I know. I know it's not.'

Part 1 – Anniversary

This is what I needed to hear.

Someone to acknowledge the severity and truth of this situation we are in. Someone to recognise and confirm what I am feeling inside yet trying so hard to keep hidden. Someone to sit with me in truth, right where I am.

I have all these people around me trying to comfort me, doing the best they can possibly do in this unchartered, terrifying situation, telling me everything is going to be ok, when I know it is not ok and nothing will ever be the same again.

NOTHING about what is happening is ok!

So, we sit.

Until I can sit no more.

I start pacing the hallway again.

I pray in my head, and I pace.

I'm screaming on the inside. I cannot describe this feeling in words, but it's like one big jumbled up internal mess and I'm unable to make sense or reason of anything.

I want to run, but know I can't.

Rob approaches me and looks me in the eye. 'Do you know what today is?' he asks.

How would I have any idea what day it is right now?

'It's Mary-Ann's anniversary.'

A wave of nausea comes over me. Pins and needles move through me as I feel like every drop of blood is being drained from my body. I lean against the wall. This is all too much to take in.

No! This cannot be happening on this day. This is not good. You can't be serious? Not this day, I think, silently.

Mary-Ann was Rob's younger sister. On this night, 7th June, sixteen years earlier, Mary-Ann had her life taken in a horrific car crash, a tragedy that left Rob and his family to pick up the pieces of their own lives. She was only twenty-four years old.

How could this be happening on the same night?

Please—someone just tell me what the hell is happening to my daughter!

This feels like some sort of horrible curse.

My thoughts drift and I take myself back to the moment when Ella was born.

Reflection Song: Girl—SYML

4

Labour Day

'The gift of life is so precious that we should feel an obligation to pay back the universe for the gift of being alive.'
Ray Bradbury

September 2003

On September 11, 2003, I was taken to our local hospital to be induced into labour to give birth to my third child. The pregnancy had been challenging, with the children's father working away, the strain of raising my two boys, aged eight and five, and numerous admissions to hospital with placenta previa and signs of early labour. The only explanation anyone ever gave me was 'having a very irritable uterus', whatever that means! All of this resulted in repeatedly being sent home to wait for it to happen all over again and wonder when this baby would actually be born. It was exhausting!

I'd be lying if I didn't say I was well and truly over being pregnant. It had been a real struggle. I loved the thought of being pregnant, but being pregnant did not love me back!

At twenty-nine years old, I knew this would be my last pregnancy. I gave birth to my first son, Sam, when I was twenty-one years old—twelve months after having half my reproductive system removed due to severe endometriosis and gynaecological issues. Told I may never be able to have children, falling pregnant with Sam was an amazing gift, unbelievable at the time. Bringing him into the world at such a young age was beautiful and scary. I would not change any of it for the world.

After experiencing a miscarriage before the birth of my second son, Timothy, when I was twenty-three, I felt even more blessed to have been given the chance to have another child, a little brother for Sam.

I'd always wanted three children, and although my pregnancy with Ella wasn't planned, we were extremely excited to be welcoming another precious child into our lives.

With my history of severe endometriosis, adenomyosis, a retroverted uterus and too many surgeries to count, I had managed to fall pregnant easily with all my children. I remember at the time of my miscarriage being told how lucky I was to have had 'one child' with my history. I acknowledged that and felt very grateful for what I had, but in my heart, I knew that was not the end of my childbearing days.

My obstetrician at the time also told me, 'You do not lose a healthy baby.' That stuck with me, something I have never forgotten. I believe this was one of the things that helped me to get through the loss of my baby after my miscarriage and be able to find some sort of acceptance of the loss.

I never allowed the words spoken to me at such a young age about the possibility of me not being able to have children to bother me. I always had a sense of knowing deep within me that things would work out exactly how they were meant to. There was a determined (and often stubborn) part of me that believed I could do anything, and I had the fortitude to prove that to myself. I would set my mind on something, visualise it, believe it would happen and do everything in my power to move towards that goal. I wanted to create a beautiful life.

There were times things didn't happen the way I'd visualised, for sure, but each time I tried, I knew I was building strength and resilience during the process for the next challenge that may come my way.

Positivity and optimism were important qualities I needed in my life.

Little did I know what I was being prepared for and why I would need this so much more in years to come.

As I was taken into the labour ward to be induced, they let me know they were extremely busy. It was September after all—nine months after Christmas—when a lot of babies enter the world. Gel was applied to my cervix to get things started and I was taken back to the ward. I sent my husband home to look after the boys, telling him I'd call if anything progressed.

I was induced early with all three of my children, due to me going into false labour so many times and nothing eventuating. I'd have loved to experience the process of going into labour naturally, but that was not on the radar for me. All night I had cramping and contractions, but nothing regular, just uncomfortable, which of course meant no sleep.

The next morning, it was back to the labour ward to have my waters broken. For some reason, it was horribly painful and brought me to tears. One of my dear friends, Liz, a midwife at the hospital, was with me. I hoped she'd be present to deliver my little girl.

Yes, I knew I was having a girl. Apart from my mum, no one else knew—not even my husband, Craig. He didn't want to know, so I kept it a secret, along with the little stash of pink clothes I hid in the back of the nursery wardrobe. I also knew that sometimes they could be wrong with the prediction of sex on ultrasounds. To me, it didn't matter if I had a boy or a girl, as long as the baby was healthy and well.

There was also the fact that on Craig's side of the family, there hadn't been a girl born for five generations. I certainly didn't want them thinking I was having a girl, then being disappointed if I popped out another boy. So, the secret was kept.

Deep down, I was so excited that I would now be blessed with a daughter to love and cherish, a little girl to share so much of my life with and make our family complete. It felt like such a blessing. I knew she would be spoilt rotten and ever so loved by her dad and two brothers. Not to mention over protected—I am sure!

I called Craig, who had dropped the boys at school, and told him to come straight to the hospital. He stopped off at the local newsagent to have a chat, let them know we were having a baby today and buy some magazines for his day hanging out in the labour ward. Unbeknown to him, I pretty much went into full labour moments after my waters were broken. It didn't take him long to realise this as he entered the room. I think he knew there was a fair chance those magazines weren't going to get read!

The pain came quickly and intensely. Liz checked me and told me I was only a couple of centimeters dilated. 'Holy shit! How am I going to handle this intensity all day? This is insane!'

As Liz's shift was finishing and she had worked all night, I told her to go home and get some sleep and I'd get one of the midwives to call her when I was getting closer. She reluctantly agreed.

My mum arrived. This was the first time she'd been present at any of my births. I felt like I wanted to give her the opportunity to be there with me and witness the miracle of a baby being born.

Part 1 – Labour Day

I remember when I was only seventeen years old, my best friend, at only sixteen, gave birth to a baby boy. She had asked me to be present with her during the birth. It was the most extraordinary, magical experience I've ever had the honour of witnessing and I'll never forget it as long as I live. It is a true gift to be present at the moment another human enters the world, and even more significant if it's being delivered by someone you love. I'll never forget the euphoria, the overwhelming surge of emotion and how it touched my heart and soul deeply. In my eyes, it was a true miracle.

As my contractions intensified quickly, I managed to make my way to the shower to try and get some relief from the warm water. I stood, holding up the bathroom wall as the hot water ran over my protruding belly. I think my mum thought I was going to cook the baby and suggested that maybe I move out of the shower. Not the best thing to tell a woman in full labour! She was probably lucky I was unable to speak due to the pain! I pressed the buzzer and a midwife entered, announcing that I was about to give birth. There was no time to call Liz.

Mum found it hard to see me in so much pain and had to leave the room for a while—but she came back.

There in that room at Maitland Hospital, Ella Kate was born, in less than an hour of me going into full labour. As she was placed on my chest, she let out a cry.

I asked if she was a girl, just to confirm. Yes, yes, she certainly was. I had my little girl.

She arrived in this world in a hurry, making sure everyone could hear her little voice.

She was perfect.

Craig went to pick Sam and Tim up from school. They arrived with so much love and joy in their young eyes as they carefully held their little sister in their arms.

I watched from a distance, exhausted and in shock after the very quick labour, my body trying to find some balance in the space, knowing in my heart and soul that our family was now complete.

Reflection Song: Life—Sleeping at Last

5

The Circle of Life

> *'The beauty of life is, while we cannot undo what is done, we can see it, understand it, learn from it, and change, so that every new moment is spent not in regret, guilt, fear, or anger, but in wisdom, understanding and love.'*
>
> Jennifer Edwards
> *When Angels Cry, A Novel*
> (2014, Yucca Publishing)

As the years passed, our little family experienced many challenges and changes. We moved to the South Coast of NSW when Ella was only a few months old, away from all our friends and family, so Craig could be closer to work. He'd been travelling back and forth for a while, causing a lot of strain on our relationship and our family unit. We needed to be together.

It seemed the logical thing to do and made sense, in order for us to stay connected. I even thought it might bring us closer together, as we'd have to rely on each other more. However, after six months, the strain of bringing up three children in a town where I knew no one, a husband working shift work, a very unsettled baby, and an equally stressed mother on the brink of having a breakdown, we decided it was best for us to move back home to be near family who could provide us with the love and support we so needed.

In our hearts, we knew there was no easy solution to the issues in our relationship, and even after moving back into our family home, having rented it out during our six-month absence, things were still not great between us.

We were both doing our best with what we knew at the time. It wasn't the first time we'd experienced problems in our marriage; they were just accumulating and not really being addressed, even though we'd been to see counsellors numerous times to work on different issues.

When I think back now to the start of our relationship, it was a bit of a whirlwind. We were young, having fun and enjoying life when I was faced with decisions about my health that I felt too young to be making at the age of twenty. I had several gynaecological problems and disorders and had already had a few surgeries. I was living in debilitating pain. After trying numerous medications, the only other option I was given was to have my left ovary and fallopian tube removed—a huge decision to have to make at that age. I did not know when I was going to have children, but I knew I couldn't continue to live with those conditions and have any quality of life. At that time in my life I had no idea there might be alternative options.

So, just a few months into our relationship, I was lying in a hospital bed after a six-hour operation to remove half my reproductive system (which had become fused to my bowel), in intense pain, not knowing if I would ever become a mum. So many emotions and stories ran through my mind while I desperately hoped I had made the right decision.

Flowers arrived. A huge bunch of roses delivered to my room with no name? Craig, of course. There was no one else in my life at the time who would do that.

Three months later I was pregnant with our first child, Sam. Not really part of the plan (not that there ever was one), but it did feel like an amazing gift. We moved in together and spent the next eight months preparing for our new family life. Still getting to know each other, we dealt with several pregnancy issues, along with the challenges that arise in new relationships—especially ones where you are about to become parents in a very short period of time.

When I look back on all of this and put it into perspective, I wonder how we lasted as long as we did. We did love each other, and we loved our children, so we did what we could to make it work the best way we knew how.

I acknowledge through reflection how challenging so many relationships are. We come together, often from two very different backgrounds and families, with our own values and conditioning, expecting to have harmonious relationships and agree on how to raise our own children together. All while maintaining a connection strong enough to get us through all of that, not forgetting the added burden of dealing with the baggage carried from childhood and past relationships that we have never processed.

It is not an easy road.

Not one to back down on a challenge, we decided to give it a red-hot go and jumped in with two feet. We got married on 2nd November 1996, when Sam was eighteen months old, I was twenty-two and Craig was twenty-five. It was a beautiful wedding, with over 160 guests. We had a lot of friends, and it became more like a huge party really! It was so much fun.

We honeymooned in Tasmania, which turned into a disaster with Sam becoming violently ill and hospitalised, followed by Craig doing the same and us flying home early. That was the beginning of our marriage.

Craig knew how to provide for his family, and that's what he did. He held down numerous jobs, working on weekends and often away. His goal was to take care of us financially and create the best possible future for us to feel secure. I knew how to care for and look after people, and that's what I did. I looked after my children and husband and gave them all the love I had, while working part-time and looking after our home.

We were trying to build our future with the tools that we had—tools that had been passed down to us through generations.

We first separated for a period of six months when Tim was two and Sam was five. I knew there was no other option at the time; however, after that break we decided to give it another go. We both dearly wanted our little family to stay together and for things to be different for us. We tried, but sometimes wanting something badly is not enough for things to change, and actions always speak louder than words. Changing ingrained patterns takes commitment and hard work. Life was busy and we were both young, going through the motions of what we thought had to be done. Things weren't always bad, we had some great times, but we were struggling, and it got to a stage where the good times no longer outweighed the bad. Then we fell pregnant for the fourth time, giving birth to Ella in September 2003.

We managed to sustain our relationship for almost eleven years in total, until it was at breaking point and we separated for good when Ella was two years old. Neither of us were happy. The energy between us was tense and impossible to hide from our children. Even so, the decision was not taken lightly. It was hard and heartbreaking.

We felt we had tried everything in search of a solution—from therapies to uprooting our whole family to a different location. However, it was not to be, and we decided it was best for our children to be living with one happy parent than in a strained household with two unhappy parents. We wanted the best for them, and for both of us as adults.

It was a very challenging time, but we kept our relationship as parents as open as possible for the sake of the children and tried hard to work together for our own sanity and peace. I believe we did the best we could for our children in every circumstance.

Years went by and we both remarried. I'm happy to say that through all our trials and tribulations, we still stay in touch and communicate with each other. We will always have a connection that can never be broken—we created our children, bringing three amazing little humans into the world who would not be here if we hadn't spent that time together.

This is part of what has made us the people we are today and one of the reasons we were brought together in the first place.

Song: Fix You—Coldplay

6

Ella's Parents

*'There are defining moments in life that leave
you breathless, frozen in time. Your life becomes
divided distinctly into two parts and nothing is
ever the same again.'*
Kim Cameron

June 2014

The doors of the Intensive Care Unit open. The neurosurgeon stands there, 'Can I see Ella's parents?'

I hasten my steps down the hallway I've been pacing. He leads us into a room where three people sit. I'm not sure who they all are? Craig and I sit down. For a split second, I wonder why there are so many people in this room? Now my full attention is on the neurosurgeon as he starts to tell us the details of the surgery he's been performing on our daughter for the past few hours. He explains what was done, what they found, and then tells us he has the worst news possible.

Is Ella in a coma? Are they not sure what damage has been done to her brain until she wakes up? This is the worst news I can think of in this moment.

I wait for these words, but they do not come.

'I am so sorry to tell you this. Ella did not survive the surgery.'

Time stands still.

WHAT did he just say?
Is this some sort of joke?
I feel like I stop breathing.
Those words can't be real.
There's no way this can be true.
It can't.
I look at him and want him to take it back.

I look at Craig. In as much shock as me, he has his head in his hands. I am desperately searching to make eye contact with him so he can tell me this is not true, so he can fix it.

Someone fix this!

I'm looking for someone, anyone, to stop what is happening as the minutes unfold in this tiny room.

There is no one.

No one is going to take back those words.

No one is going to make this go away.

No one is going to bring my daughter back.

I'm trying to understand what he's just said.

Surely this can't be real?

I don't know what to do. We're both in shock, devastated, unable to fully comprehend the magnitude of what we've just been told.

I sit at Craig's feet. I don't know why. I don't know what else to do.

It feels instinctual, yet out of desperation at the same time.

This is our daughter. I just want him to tell me this is all a bad dream.

He doesn't.

Standing up, I turn to the surgeon. The only words that come out of my mouth are, 'This is bullshit!'

Now I'm pacing the tiny little room—in full denial of what is happening.

I want to escape. Run. Get out of here. Get away from this moment in time so it can all disappear and we can rewind our lives back a day, half a day even.

I feel like I've been dragged out of my own reality and into some crazy realm that now has control over me physically, emotionally, and mentally.

He's still talking to us.

He tells us how sorry he is and how they did everything they could to save our little girl.

I can't hear what he is saying now.

I can't even look at him.

I am no longer in my own body.

This can't be real. It just can't. Children don't just die. Not my children. Not my beautiful, healthy children.

How can this be happening?

Five hours ago, my little girl was laughing, smiling, and dancing—now I'm being told that her life has ended. Just like that.

NO.

Minutes feel like hours.

I want to scream, but nothing comes out.

I don't know what to do. I have no control over what has happened. I can't change it. I can't make it better.

There is nothing I can do. Nothing!

I sit in silence.

Just when I think this can't get any worse, it does.

My husband, Craig's wife and our two boys are called into the room.

Oh my god, this is too overwhelming! How do I look at these three men in my life as they all walk into this room at the same time and are told the same dreaded news that we have just been crushed by?

I don't know who to go to first.

I need Rob to hold me, to tell me everything is going to be ok—when I clearly know it isn't.

I need to hold my boys, to tell them everything is going to be ok—which they clearly know it's not by the tears streaming down my face.

This is way too much to deal with and I cannot change any of it. Not for anyone.

Everything feels out of control.

I am worried about all of them.

There are now nine people in this little room.

Shock, tears, wailing, disbelief, denial, pain and confusion are all present, along with the compassionate surgeon who did everything in his power to save our daughter.

Someone asks if we want to see Ella.

Yes, yes, I need to be with my little girl. Where is she?

Yet the thought of it takes my breath away.

Oh my god, how am I going to do this?

The surgeon leaves the room to ensure she is out of theatre, and we are taken to a curtained-off area in a large ward. There is no one else here but us.

There is nothing comforting about any of this.

It feels cold and stark.

As I walk through the curtain there is my precious baby girl, lying lifeless on a hospital bed.

The reality of what we've been told hits hard, like I'm walking head-on into a brick wall.

I feel like I am crumbling away from the inside out.

Oh, my darling Ella, how can this be?

WHY?

Tears flow uncontrollably as my heart feels like it's being torn out of my chest.

I look at her beautiful innocent face, her blue eyes closed, never to open again. I see how hard they've worked to save her precious life.

Why did she have to go through such trauma and pain? Why couldn't they save her? Why?

I focus on the dressing over the left side of her head, covering the area where they had desperately entered her brain trying to stop the bleeding. *What happened inside there, my beautiful girl?*

I want to be able to say she looks peaceful, but it's hard for me to see this. All I can see is her exhausted little body that tried so hard to hang on to life. Her heart stopping once during surgery, only to be brought back to life once more as she tried so hard to hold on for as long as she possibly could.

Until she couldn't.

I know how hard she would have fought, until it all became too much for her little body and her heart stopped beating again for the second time.

The last time.

Her beautiful, gentle, loving heart could not take any more.

I kiss her gently and tell her how much I love her and how sorry I am, over and over again.

What did I do wrong?

'I'm so sorry, Ella.'

I was meant to protect you, that's what mums do. Protect their babies. Nurture them. Safeguard them from danger.

The tears won't stop.

I don't think they ever will.

Why did this have to happen to her? She didn't deserve to have her short, precious life ended in this way. There are no answers. No justification for what has happened here.

This is a pain that will never go away. Ever.

Seeing my child's lifeless body and knowing I will never get to hold her, speak with her or give her the life I had dreamed of is like being physically and emotionally tortured all at once. The feelings are so deep, so raw and intense. I'm not even sure there are words in the English language to describe the darkness of this moment in its full depth.

My whole body starts shaking. Dry retching, I grab a laundry trolley to hold onto. I don't know how to navigate through this. There is no resilience to draw on. No strength. There is nothing. Every bit of hope I'd been holding onto is gone.

I am in shock.

Hurting.

Numb.

Distraught.

I am in a place I've never been before.

I am in survival mode.

Rob is with me, processing his own grief and pain, while trying to support me in this unknown territory both of us have now entered. We slowly walk back into the room where we were initially told the devastating news. The doctor asks if we would like to speak to our family in person or if we would like him to. There are around eight family members still outside in the waiting room. Our parents—Ella's grandparents. Our siblings—Ella's aunties and uncles.

This is not something Craig or I feel we can do. It is just too much to cope with—having to see them experience the same shock of what we have just been told and are trying to process in some kind of way. Even though I am in my own world of grief and shock, and everything that goes along with it, I'm worried about everyone else. I'm concerned about the impact this news is going to have on my family. My sister is five months pregnant, and my mum has already experienced the loss of her only sister nine years earlier in very similar circumstances.

We're sitting in the same room we sat in when we had to make the horrible decision to turn off my auntie's life support machine weeks after her surgery, only now we've been told our only daughter has died.

I cannot comprehend life at all right now.

The surgeon goes out to inform our family while we sit silently in this room, together—yet so far apart in our own worlds of distraught heartache. Not knowing what to do next.

I hold on to my boys' hands.

Then we hear it—the wailing, the distraught screaming, the tears from the other side of the wall. It is too much to bear. The pain from my family feels like it's seeping into my bones. My crying is so intense, from a place I didn't know existed, and I don't know what to do. My own pain is hard enough for me to hold. The intensity of the pain around me feels unbearable.

I feel my boys' pain and my heart breaks even more. I hold them tight. How will we survive this?

There are no rules here.

No guidebook to follow.

What are we meant to do now?

Eventually, we settle ourselves as best we can, knowing we must walk out through those doors to face our families. This is hard—really hard.

No one knows what to say.

No one knows what to do.

I don't want to make eye contact with anyone.

Being held by those who love me, although probably what I need the most, brings me to my knees. I have never felt this depth of pain.

A part of me still feels I must stay strong for my boys, but I am not sure I can do that. Oh, my poor boys. This is not right. They had spent the day together with Ella, just like any other normal day, with Sam going off to his girlfriend's house in the afternoon and Tim to his part-time job—Ella telling him she loved him as he walked out the door. Never in their worst nightmares could they have known they would never see their little sister alive again.

It's time to leave the hospital.

Without Ella…

Walking slowly through the corridors, I feel broken and numb. The exit doors loom in front of me. I just want to turn around and run back to her. How can I leave her alone, by herself? How can I walk out these front doors into the world I don't know how to function in without one of my children?

I want to take her home.

I glance at the hospital chapel on the left as I walk past, the place I longed to sit while Ella was in surgery, to beg God to save my little girl.

I feel nothing.

What sort of God would take the life of an innocent child?

I don't understand…

I hate you.

We're in the car now for the drive home. My heart aches and breaks uncontrollably. My head is in a jumbled mess of confusion and disbelief. Suddenly, the numbness starts moving through me again.

We drive home in silence.

No words.

Just tears.

What the hell just happened?

Reflection Song: I Want You Here—Plumb

7

The Front Door

'When the links of life are broken and a child has to part, there is nothing that will ever heal a parent's broken heart.'
Author Unknown

We're home. I don't want to get out of the car.

It's now very early in the morning. Rob's parents are waiting for us in their car on the front lawn.

When I finally get out of the car, they meet us on our front porch. They hug us. They know this pain all too well. They know the pain of losing their only daughter, their youngest child. I cannot look them in the eyes. I can feel their own pain and their compassion for me in their embrace. I'm not sure they can look me in the eyes either. It's way too painful for everyone.

I look at the front door. It's not the same.

Nothing will ever be the same again behind this door.

Rob places the key in the lock and turns it.

He opens the door and waits for me to go inside.

I step inside slowly.

What are we meant to do?

We try to comfort each other in some way, but our bodies are in shock and we can't really function. I hold my boys tightly, before they make their way to their bedrooms to try and process in some way what the hell has just happened to our family. There is nothing I can do to take their pain away or mine.

I can't bear the thought of walking into Ella's bedroom. So, I go to my room and lie on my bed, curling myself up into a ball. Rob holds me.

I cry uncontrollably.

We cry. For what feels like hours. Eventually, we fall asleep out of exhaustion.

Waking suddenly, I find two hours have passed.

I turn to Rob, my eyes wide, pleading with him to tell me this isn't real—that last night did not happen. I beg him to tell me this was all a nightmare. And just for a fleeting moment, I think it is. I look at him in desperation.

Please tell me she is still here, that she is going to walk through that bedroom door any minute and climb into bed with us.

He doesn't.

He can't.

I can't move from my bed. I want to feel nothing, but I feel everything, and it feels like my chest is being crushed. It's crippling. I can't function.

I get Rob to check on the boys. I'm so concerned and worried for them, what must they be going through at just sixteen and nineteen years of age, losing their little sister who they adored.

How was I going to get myself through this, let alone them?

Less than twelve hours ago my daughter was alive and happy—and now she is gone.

Her death, so sudden and unexpected, gave us no time for preparation or goodbyes, leaving us all shell shocked.

It's said that bad news travels fast. In no time, our home is filled with family and friends. They're all in shock, all with broken hearts for Ella and our family.

After a while, I manage to move from my bed to the lounge, where I just sit, more out of a feeling of obligation to those coming to see me and pay their respects than being what I actually want to do. They try to comfort me in any way they feel they can.

Sometimes it's good to have people here I can connect with, talk to and go over and over the events that have taken place, trying to make some sense of what is happening.

It feels like this has been going on for days on end as the exhaustion comes and goes. Other times, I just want everyone to go away.

I fluctuate between trying to keep it all together and totally falling apart. From bed to lounge. Lounge to bed.

As comforting as bed is, it's also a very lonely and often scary place to be once everyone leaves each day. Reality is always looming, just waiting for me to connect to it as it prepares to tear my heart out all over again.

There are times I just want to be alone.

In those quiet moments as the days pass, I slowly make my way into Ella's room. The first time I tell myself I am brave enough to go in there, my hand covers my mouth as I stand in the doorway in disbelief.

The pain is unbearable.

I sit on her floor, broken and distraught. Holding on tightly to her treasured toys. Smelling her pyjamas. Looking at the hair in her hairbrush. Clinging to every tiny thing I have left of her, which is never going to be enough.

I am angry because her sheets got washed and changed the day she went to her dad's. I want to lie in her bed and smell her.

I don't want clean sheets.

I don't know how to get close enough to her. Nothing is going to be enough.

I worry constantly about my boys. They both have beautiful girlfriends to lean on for comfort and support, for which I am ever so grateful, but the girls are also grieving the loss of Ella, who they both considered their own little sister. Ella thought it was fantastic to have other girls in the house, and I know for sure that at times the boys had to compete with Ella for time with their own girlfriends.

But now, I know they would all do anything to spend another moment with her. What anyone would give to watch her favourite movie *Frozen* with her just one more time, even though we swore we never wanted to see it again.

Everyone is in so much pain.

Reflection Song: Jealous of the Angels—Donna Taggart

8

Goodbye

'And then she moved from shock to grief the way she might enter another room.'
Anita Shreve
The Pilot's Wife
(2014, Abacus)

It's time to make the preparations for Ella's farewell. It takes me a couple of days before I can even pick up the phone to ring the funeral home. A call I never imagined I would ever have to make.

This is not the natural order of death. Parents are supposed to die before their children. Children bury their parents. Parents are not meant to bury their children.

I don't know how any of this is meant to work. I close the door to my bedroom and sit on the side of my bed, alone, holding Ella's favourite stuffed toy 'Woofy', a cuddly dog with big floppy ears, close to my chest. My body rocks back and forth as it tries to comfort itself once more in some way. I dial the number and listen to the sound of the phone ringing in my ear. Someone answers. I am meant to talk.

What do I say?

I don't know what to say or how to say it.

I don't want to say it.

Saying those words makes it so real. I don't want this to be real.

I don't want to bury my daughter.

'Um, hello.'

'Hello, can I help you?'

I swallow hard and try to find the words.

'My daughter passed away.' That is all I can get out.

The tears roll down my cheeks uncontrollably as the pain inside my body intensifies.

The words sting and cut deep, like a knife twisting into my heart.

They are so caring and considerate of my broken heart and know just what to say and what to do. This is their job. Every day they speak to grieving families, and I am no different. Although it is so hard for me to recognise myself as one of these people, I can certainly feel it.

As broken as I am, I feel so distraught for other parents I know who have lost their children. Their children who never got to go to school, or finish school, or get a job, or get married, or have their own children, or live out their dreams. Their children who were taken away from them, way too soon.

Why did they have to experience this pain?

It's like being part of a club that you never wanted to join at any cost.

It's a transition into a new reality that I can only imagine will take time, a very long time.

Ella was a child and died in a hospital, which means there has to be an investigation into her death. A mandatory procedure, that resulted in us having to wait almost two weeks to say our final goodbyes. Although this feels like a long time, it will give us space to plan the celebration of Ella's life. It is so important to me that it has special meaning for us, our family, her friends and for Ella.

I think about how often farewell services are held so quickly, so close to the time a person dies—as though this could be some sort of closure or ending to what you are feeling. I know it must happen, and is part of the process, but what is the hurry about—really?

Is it so everyone can get on with their lives once the funeral is over? I don't think so. Not for those who are broken. Having the extra time to spend processing our own thoughts, emotions and feelings, taking time to reflect on what is important to say or do and feeling into how we want to honour the one we love so dearly cannot be rushed. This process needs to be slow.

We've decided not to have Ella's service in a church. We want her farewell to be a celebration of her life, focussing on nothing but her. Her service is to be held in a beautiful private chapel in Newcastle. We visit the chapel to make sure it feels right. As I sit listening to details being discussed, it all becomes too much for me. I feel overwhelmed with despair and cannot comprehend why we are here.

We shouldn't be here. This is not how it is meant to be.

Tears stream down my face. Devastated. Angry. I want to run.

I don't want to be here.

I don't want to be responsible for organising this.

I don't want to say goodbye to my only daughter.

I don't want to watch my two sons go through this pain.

I don't want this to be my reality.

But it doesn't really matter what I don't want, because I have all of this right here in front of me and I can't close my eyes and sleep long enough for it to all go away.

I feel like I am suffocating; it is so hard to breathe.

What colour casket would you like?

What sort of flowers do you want?

Do you want balloons?

What songs do you want played?

Do you want a photo slide show?
Who will speak?
Who will carry her little coffin out of the chapel?
Do you want transport? Who will travel in the cars?
I don't fucking know! I just want my daughter back.

I walk outside to get some fresh air and wish the ground would open and swallow me up. But it doesn't!

Eventually, I go back inside to face the inevitable. I hug Rob and my boys. I answer what questions I can, together with Ella's dad. We decide she will be buried at a small local cemetery that overlooks some paddocks, near our homes. It feels like a quiet and peaceful place and there are horses—she loved horses.

On the morning of Ella's funeral, I wake up and my heart is out of rhythm. This is not the first time this has happened.

Please God, not today. Give me a break.

I wait to see if it will go back into a normal rhythm by itself. It doesn't, so I have to go to the hospital. I cannot believe this is happening! At the hospital I am wired up, with a crash cart on standby as they give me a dose of Adenosine—an antiarrhythmic agent used to treat Paroxysmal Supraventricular Tachycardia (PVST), a condition I have. This drug has a very short half-life in human blood (less than ten seconds). The effects slow down the heart quickly, enough to reset the electrical rhythm back to normal sinus rhythm. I hate having this drug injected. It's scary and feels horrid, like the drug takes over my whole body, sucking the life out of me, before I gasp for air as my heart resets itself and I hope that it has gone back into a normal rhythm. A flood of emotion usually follows which I have no control over.

Part 1 – Goodbye

Rob is by my side, as always, holding my hand. He knows how scary this is for me and I know how scary it is for him. He watches the screen as they inject the drug and my heart rate flatlines for a few seconds. I'm sure he is not breathing at this stage. After this intense, quick procedure is over, I see the tears rolling down his cheek as he holds me and reassures me I am ok through my own tears. My heart has reset. I usually have to stay for a few hours to be monitored after this, but once the situation is explained to the doctor, they keep me for a short time and let me go home on the promise I will come back if it goes out of rhythm again.

I have had this procedure done four times in the last year and it is starting to take its toll. I've been told I cannot keep having this drug injected regularly and am scheduled to have surgery later this year to try to block an extra pathway I have in my heart that is contributing to this problem.

Exhausted, I just want to go home to my boys, who are now worrying about me while having to process the fact that they are about to bury their little sister today.

It's all too much.

We've organised a limousine to take us all to the chapel so we can be together, my husband and I, Craig and his wife and our two boys. One of the things Ella is certainly making sure of is that she is bringing us all closer together, something I know she always wanted.

The heavy feeling in my stomach gets deeper as the limousine pulls up outside the funeral home. There are so many people they overflow outside. Feeling like everyone is watching us as we get out of the car, I realise the magnitude of what we are about to walk into. Breathing deeply, I walk through the crowd of people, my hand in Rob's, my boys behind me, towards the front of the room where Ella's white coffin sits, adorned in flowers that I cannot see any beauty in today.

It's hard to breathe. This makes everything so real. So final.

It's like being forced to be somewhere you don't want to be, yet know you have to be. I sit as close to her as I can, knowing I have to get through this.

The first thing that plays on the large video screen at the beginning of the service is a Singstar video Ella made of herself dancing and miming the song *Roar* by Katy Perry. I watch her with tears falling from my eyes as she tells everyone in that room that she is a champion and shows us her muscles. Watching her full of life doing what she loved makes my heart ache so deeply. Knowing she will never have the chance to do this on this earth and that our home will never be filled with her voice or laughter ever again is torturous.

Craig and I stand together at the pulpit as he reads the eulogy we've written together in memory of our beautiful daughter. I don't think I can speak in front of the hundreds of people standing before us. I have spoken at many of my family's funerals before, but this, I cannot bring myself to do. I place my hand on Craig's arm for support as he struggles to get the words out. I remind him to breathe. We may have been divorced for seven years, but here we stand united as Ella's biological mother and father. Broken, lost, connected in a way we never imagined in our worst nightmares, doing our best to pay tribute to our little girl.

Tim stands with Sam as he reads a poem he and Ella had read at mine and Rob's wedding only seventeen months earlier. Watching Sam read this poem with Tim by his side,

I imagine Ella standing there with them both and my heart breaks open a little more.

A Family
A family is a place where you can cry and laugh,
Be silly or sad, or cross,
Where you can ask for help,
Tease and yell at each other,
And know that you will always be loved.

A family is made up of people who care about you when you're sad,
Who love you all the time, no matter what.
They don't expect you to be perfect,
They just want you to try to be the best you can be.

A family is a safe place,
Where we learn to like ourselves,
And learn what love is all about.
We learn how to deal with life,
To prepare ourselves for the world.

The world is a place where anything can happen.
If we grow up in a loving family like mine,
We are ready for the world.
Author Unknown

Well, my beautiful girl, I hope you are ready for your new world, because I am certainly not ready for mine. While this poem is an important part of our family and what we believe in, it's hard to imagine that anything could have prepared us for what we are going through.

You Are My Sunshine plays (the song I sang to Ella at night before she fell asleep) as images of her beautiful life roll across the screen. How can this even be real?

Craig, Rob, Sam and Tim carry her little white coffin out of the chapel.

Unconditionally by Katy Perry plays. Ella loved Katy Perry.

The sight of these brave, broken boys and men, who all hold different parts of my heart, carrying my daughter in their arms is gut-wrenchingly painful.

I hear the words of the song echo through my mind, words about acceptance and freedom.

I don't know how to do this, but I will do my best, baby girl.

There are images and moments in life that feel like they have been carved into your soul with a knife. This is one of them.

Seeing Ella's beautiful little friends with their broken hearts is so hard to witness. It's like I'm feeling my pain and theirs all at once. I keep imagining in my mind that they are Ella and that she has lost one of her dear friends. I know how distraught she would be. These little children shouldn't have to experience this pain at such a young age.

How unprepared we are in our culture to deal with death of any kind. We don't talk about it often, yet it is something we will all experience. It is inevitable. When faced with tragic, unpredictable circumstances, no one has time to prepare themselves or say goodbye, making it even harder to process and understand.

Why do we think we always have more time?

Reflection Song: Unconditionally—Katy Perry

9

Treading Water

'There is no footprint too small to leave an imprint on this world.'
Author Unknown

So many of Ella's friends come to visit me, giving me precious hugs, cards, drawings and gifts in memory of Ella, and it means the world to me. It is important for me that they have the opportunity to be involved in Ella's farewell, so we had them write messages to Ella on pieces of paper which the celebrant read out. This was accompanied by special messages from her cousins, whom she loved dearly. They were just as young as her, and even younger.

So many people's lives are forever changed on this day.

Driving to the cemetery where Ella is to be laid to rest, a forty-minute drive from the chapel but only ten minutes from our home, we are all together in the limousine, this time joined by Sam and Tim's girlfriends. We play Katy Perry, for Ella, but it's just not the same. It will never be the same again. We are trying hard, but it all just feels so forced and wrong. This is all we can do in the midst of the heartbreak and confusion we're all feeling.

More words are spoken, and music is played as everyone gathers around the gravesite. Family lay rainbow roses on her casket. The celebrant looks to me to see if I am ready to have the coffin lowered.

I am never going to be ready for this.

I step forward, as close as I can get to the deep, dark hole in the ground. Rob moves to be by my side to hold me. I think he is genuinely worried about how close I am as he lovingly asks me to step back with him. I am not moving. No one is going to move me right now. All I want to do is jump in this hole with her. I'm sure he can sense what I'm feeling.

The coffin lowers into the ground. As I feel my body crumble on the inside, Rob holds me up.

I visualise my precious baby girl's lifeless body lying in there, so beautiful, peaceful, her long blonde hair, her beautiful blue eyes closed gently. She has her favourite new, soft-yellow floral dress draped over her body. Her sparkly silver shoes adorn her small feet. Her favourite stuffed toy dog is by her side, along with all the special things we have placed in there with her.

How can this be happening?

One hundred coloured balloons are released into the sky by family and friends. It is truly a beautiful farewell. I know in my heart that Ella would have loved it.

The day is long. Exhausted, now we're heading to the local golf club. Hundreds of people are here. It's overwhelming. With a large screen playing a photo story of Ella's beautiful life, it still doesn't seem real. There is no reality for me in this. Not for what has happened, or what is happening now.

In a place that feels so foreign and unknown, I feel like an alien on earth.

I sit. People bring me food I can't eat. I look around. Everyone seems to be socialising, and in an odd way, having some sort of a good time—eating, drinking, catching up with people they haven't seen in ages. It's weird for me. Hard to explain. Hard to fathom. People have travelled long distances and want to convey their condolences, which is beautiful, but so draining on my grieving, shocked body that I feel so detached from.

Finally, we're heading home. Home to this new reality that has been cruelly forced upon us.

Now what?

It's been a few weeks now since Ella's funeral. It's passed like a blur. The hordes of people have started to dwindle, and the bouquets of flowers have wilted and been thrown out. I have never felt so lost.

I cannot bring myself to go to the shops to buy groceries, or even leave the house, unless I am going to the cemetery. Ella's school is amazing. They bring our family food and cooked meals for more than a month. It is a blessing. Not to mention the meals that neighbours, friends and family keep bringing.

I need to know my boys are being taken care of and this is something I always did—now it's a struggle. I don't have the energy to take care of them but feel guilty at the same time for needing to take care of myself—with no idea how to even do that. I just do the best I can in every moment, trying to function and live in the confusing darkness that is now my life.

I make my way into Ella's bedroom daily. Looking around at every little nick-nack, drawing and piece of writing that reminds me of her. The posters on the walls. The make-believe shopping lists. The notes to friends. Her diary. Her hair bands. Her beanie bear collection. Never did I ever imagine that all these little things would hold so much value. Never did I ever think this would be all I have left of my little girl.

The emptiness I am holding is so heavy that my whole body aches.

I look at the photos she has on her wall of me and her, Sam and Tim, and remember how she would take them down randomly if she was upset with any of us. This makes me laugh inside and hurts like hell at the same time.

Everything in this room is part of who she was.

I lie in her bed, sobbing, not wanting to move. This is the closest I can get to her as I try to come to terms with the fact that I will never hold her again.

I think back to the nights at bedtime when all she wanted me to do was lie with her, hold her close, while she talked about her day, her worries, her dreams. Moments I thought we would have over and over again. The music we would always play to help her get to sleep as I stroked her hair. I close my eyes and imagine she is here in my arms. I talk to her like she is.

I open her wardrobe. My eyes scan her favourite pieces of clothing. I pick up a few, one by one, and hold them in my hands, wondering how I will ever be able to part with any of this. The days here alone are hard, but they are also the days when I allow my heart to release some of the agony it holds onto ever so tightly when other people are around. Not that I try to hide my grief, as that is not even possible, but there are times I feel I don't need to burden others with the intensity of my own pain.

I know my family and friends are worried about me. They check on me constantly with phone calls, messages and visits, but some days I just don't want to talk to anyone. Some days I just want to stay in bed.

I'm taking double the dose of my anti-anxiety mediation now. I've been taking it on and off since Ella was born as a result of the breakdown I suffered while living away from family when she was a baby. My grief for Ella became so overwhelming I didn't know how to manage it myself, so I took myself to the doctor. Doubling the dose seems to be helping, as it is much easier not to feel the intensity of everything. 'It might just help to take the edge off,' the doctor said.

The problem is exactly that—I'm not feeling everything.

Many of the emotions and feelings I have inside of me, as hard and confronting as they are, are being pushed down into my body somewhere instead of being felt. I don't realise this, I'm not aware. I just need to survive, so I keep taking them.

The stronger dose of medication and a couple of glasses of red wine each night usually means I can get a couple hours of sleep in the early hours of the morning. Waking up to another painful day of this fucked-up reality now called my life as the sun tries to creep through my windows once again, I pull the covers over my head, trying desperately to go back to sleep. I pray the sun will go away and allow me to sleep for just a little while longer—in a place where I can't feel anything.

Along with the sun come the committed friends and family who keep appearing, determined not to see me drown in my grief. My sister Kylie is a lifeline, showing up every day for me in whatever way she can. She is trying to process her own pain of losing her only niece, while caring for her two children who've just lost their cousin, as they try to understand how this could happen to another child, and one they loved so dearly. All this, while being pregnant with her third child.

How do you explain to children, who saw Ella as a healthy little girl, not to be scared of dying? Many of her friends are scared, asking questions such as, 'What if I have the same thing as Ella and nobody knows? Could I die too?

Nobody knew there was anything wrong with Ella. What if this happens to me?'

There aren't many people I've asked to be here for me, they just keep coming, out of love, all so heartbroken and lost as they try to do whatever they can to console me.

My parents live between my house and theirs, which is just around the corner, processing their own grief of losing their granddaughter, while witnessing their eldest daughter go through her darkest days. My in-laws are present too, although I'm sure they are feeling the effects of compounded grief from the loss of their own daughter as they witness what Rob and I are going through. No one really knows what to say or do. We are all in unchartered waters.

Having these people, and so many more, by my side and knowing they will be here whenever I need them is such a gift. They bring me food, flowers, gifts, and anything they can think of that they feel might put a slight smile on my face for a short period of time—but most of all, they give me unconditional love. They never give up on me. Even when there's nothing anyone can say, they just sit with me, cry with me and hold my hand. And those who find this too hard to bear, keep themselves busy helping me in practical ways.

These people know who they are and do not need any recognition for their emotional courage—giving from their hearts, feeling my pain, then going home to their own children and families and questioning why.

Rob is so supportive as he navigates his way around his own emotions and mine. I know he's in a lot of pain. He's processing his own grief of losing his only stepdaughter who he loved and adored so dearly, along with the cumulative grief he has that is arising from losing his only sister sixteen years earlier. This all seems to be way too much of a coincidence. I constantly ask myself why we have been brought together to go through this. Why did he have to experience another tragic loss of one of the most important females in his life?

What is the lesson in this that we all have to learn?

One thing I know is that he understands what it's like for Sam and Tim to lose their younger sister, and if he can do anything to help them get through this in any way at all, then that will be a beautiful gift. His love for the boys and his ability to express his emotions and show affection towards them is more than enough in these moments.

Some days, the depth of my grief and despair feels like it is too much to bear as I sit on the shower floor, water falling onto my exhausted body, feeling I will never be able to get up as my tears become one with the running water, disappearing down the plug hole. Other days, everything makes me so angry I want to punch holes in the walls.

Then there's the days I totally numb out, not allowing myself to feel anything. Zombie like. Robotic. A coping mechanism. Trying not to feel at all.

The emotions are so intense at times I can't keep pushing them down, yet I have no idea what to do with them.

I feel so lost and alone.

Something inside of me tells me it's time to get some help.

Reflection Song: The Next Right Thing—Kristen Bell

Part 2

10
Vilomah

'If you know someone who has lost a child, and you are afraid to mention them because you think it might make them sad by reminding them that they died—you're not reminding them. They didn't forget they died.

What you are reminding them of is that you remembered that they lived, and that's a great, great gift.'
Elizabeth Edwards

When Karla Holloway, a James B. Duke professor of English at Duke University, suffered the loss of a child, she discovered there was no word that gave meaning to a parent whose child had died. To this day, there still isn't a word in the English language that is widely known, used and accepted.

If you lose your husband or wife, you're a widower or widow.

If you lose your parents, you're an orphan.

But how do you describe yourself to someone when you've lost a child?

If this was your only child, does it mean you are no longer a parent?

How would you tell people you were once a parent, but now you are not?

It's hard enough to find meaning in this cruel new reality you're experiencing, let alone having to struggle to describe this new way of existing to others without difficult, lengthy explanations. Not that there needs to be a label, but a word to use in these situations that neatly and respectfully describes the mess and aftermath of who you become after your child dies may just feel a little less intrusive each time it comes up.

> **'Vilomah' is a Sanskrit word that means against a natural order and is used to describe a person whose child has died. It's more than that, encompassing all that occurs and is felt when a parent loses a child.**

Sanskrit, one of the oldest known languages in the world, is found in the scriptures of Hinduism, Buddhism, and Jainism. It also gave us the word widow—which actually means empty.

Everyone's healing journey is different. Finding the right word to describe not only your pain and suffering, but who you've become after your child dies, is an important and necessary part of surviving the loss of a child for some people. Perhaps the word Vilomah will find its way into mainstream English language one day. Maybe we can all help it to get there by using it when needed and teaching others about its existence.

Let's hope we don't have to use it too often.

Who Are We?
Who are we?
We are parents,
Mums and dads.
Or are we now?

When your child
No longer walks this earth,
How do you explain
Your purpose?
How?

I am a parent.
I was a mum.
I had a daughter,
Now she is gone.

The truth so hard,
Those words to speak.
They don't want to hear them,
Happiness they seek.
                    Kim Cameron

≈

Reflection Song: Graves—Aisha Badru

11
Just Do It

'There is no reason not to follow your heart.'
Steve Jobs

A little over two years before losing Ella, I left my job to run the office at Rob's hydraulic company. I'd been working some nights and weekends to help, while holding a thirty-hour a week job as a Disability Co-ordinator and bringing up my three children. I knew something had to give. We could see the company was doing well and was going to create a secure financial future for us, so it seemed like the practical decision for us to work towards this together.

A few months before Ella left, I spoke to Rob about the lack of job satisfaction I felt, having worked in the office for almost two years (mostly in solitude). I shared with him my longing to study and change my career direction. One of our goals in our marriage was to always support each other's dreams in whatever way we could. We decided this was the best option for us, both as individuals and as a couple. We employed a new lady to run the office and I started to train her so I could leave to pursue my dream.

I'd had a strong curiosity and desire to study Holistic Kinesiology for a couple of years. My middle son, Tim, had been struggling with a lot of gastrointestinal issues, headaches, lethargy and passing out at times for no apparent reason. We'd taken him to see doctors, specialists, naturopaths, dieticians and even had blood tests sent overseas to try to establish what was going on in his then fourteen-year-old body. He was missing a lot of school, and no one could give us any answers. We tried many elimination diets, thinking he had an intolerance to certain foods, but nothing showed up. He'd seemed happy at school before this started, was active and had lots of friends, with no major issues that we knew about, so it was all a real mystery to us and was consuming our lives as we tried desperately over a long period of time to help him find some relief.

One day I took him to see a Kinesiologist. I watched in awe as she worked with him and his body, shifting energy in his stomach and bowel, checking to see where the stress lay in his body. I saw an immediate shift and he felt it. It was such a relief to see him like that. I couldn't believe the difference one session had made for him. I knew we still had a lot of work to do, but this was a start, and it opened my eyes to new possibilities.

Later that day I started to think—imagine what it would be like to be able to do something like that (Kinesiology)—not thinking I ever would, or could, for that matter.

That experience had left an imprint on my heart and resonated with me on such a deep soul level that it was impossible to shake. It had awoken something inside me that I couldn't explain. I could feel it.

I had looked into it a couple of times, but could never really see, nor justify, how I could make it work within our family unit, or how I could afford it. I would have to study some of the time in Sydney, which was two hours away. I was a mum with other responsibilities that always felt more important than what I wanted to do for myself, but the seed had been planted and was growing strong.

I made the decision to leave Rob's company and enrolled in a dual diploma to study Kinesiology and Mind Body Medicine. I would travel to Sydney two days a week to do face-to-face classes and complete the theory online from home. I had also applied for a part-time job as a Co-ordinator of Disability Services (my previous career that I loved) in Newcastle, and was to be employed two to three days a week so I had enough money to contribute to our family and be able to study.

Oh yes, I was also still running a home and bringing up three children. Rob was working long hours and was on call pretty much twenty-four hours a day, seven days a week. At the time, this all seemed achievable to me, and I was excited. Rob was supportive, as were my family. In hindsight, I have no idea how this would have ever worked or what I was thinking—this reads like a recipe for disaster and burnout!

The boys, aged sixteen and nineteen, were becoming more self-sufficient and responsible and both had part-time jobs. Tim was still at school (when he could get there) and Sam was studying at TAFE.

Ella would be turning eleven in September and was in Year 5 at school. I spoke to her about what I wanted to do. I told her how I would have to drive to Sydney two days a week and she would have to go to her Nan and Pa's house on those afternoons after school. Part of my decision to work for Rob in the first place had been to be able to be there for her each morning and afternoon to get her to school and pick her up after. This was really important for me, and I was so blessed to have that one-on-one time with her.

When I spoke to Ella, I think I was really looking for her permission. Carrying parent guilt for putting what I wanted first was hard and I wanted to make sure this was going to be ok with her. I knew she was wanting to be a little more independent as she'd asked me on numerous occasions to walk home from the bus stop by herself after school (that never happened, as I was always there waiting for her).

When I finished talking, she turned to me and said, 'Mum, is this what you really want to do?'

'Yes, sweetie, it is.'

She said, 'Well, just do it.'

To her it was a no brainer. And in that moment, I thought, *wow, out of the mouths of our children. I just need to follow my heart and 'just do it'.*

Thanks 'chicken' for the reassurance.

Two weeks later, Ella was gone.

≈

Reflection Song: The Voice Within—Christina Aguilera

12

What Are You Going To Do Now?

'You don't always need a plan. Sometimes you just need to breathe, trust, let go and see what happens.'

Mandy Hale

A few weeks after losing Ella, people started asking me what I was going to do.

What do you mean what was I 'going to do'?

I had declined the job offer as Disability Co-ordinator. There was no way I was capable of working with vulnerable people, being so vulnerable myself. I couldn't even leave the house most days, let alone try and co-ordinate someone else's life. Some thought I should try to work, that it would be a good distraction.

I didn't want a distraction. I wanted my daughter back, and as much as I knew this was never going to happen, I certainly didn't want people telling me what they thought I should do.

I was in pain and angry.

One night, Rob spoke to me about the study I had planned to do. He asked if I still wanted to do it. I guess he was wondering what I was going to do with myself too. He had to go back to work, and I knew he was worried about me. I didn't want to do anything, and I couldn't understand how or why people were trying to push me. That's what it felt like at the time.

I didn't want to move on.

How could I move on without my little girl? My family was broken.

It felt like no one understood. Like no one could feel my pain. There were many days I just wanted everyone to disappear.

It's interesting when I look back at all the things people said to me, thinking they were helping in some way—the only way they knew how. I realise now that they were all coming from a loving and caring space, but there was also fear there for them. They were scared. They were worried about me, and when I was not doing ok, neither were they.

It's hard to see someone you love hurting, especially when there is nothing you can do to make it any better.

Often, when people are crying we hand them a box of tissues. Why do we do this?

Because we want their tears and pain to stop?

Because we don't know what else to do?

Because it is often not a comfortable place for us to be in?

What would happen if we did nothing other than sit with that person in that space of pain and grief and simply be with them, meet them there. Let the tears fall freely.

Sometimes that's all I wanted—for someone to meet me there—not tell me what they thought I should do, or how if I just did something once, how much easier it would be the second time around.

Or the icing on the cake—how lucky I was to have another two children who were still alive…

It felt like no one knew how painful it was for me to go to a supermarket, where everything I used to buy for my little girl to pack her school lunch box was a trigger—the packets of snacks and sultanas, the juice boxes, the muffins—all the things that were in front of my face but no longer needed to be in my trolley.

Walking through a department store and seeing the little girls' clothing section out of the corner of my eye brought me to tears.

Seeing mothers and daughters walking hand-in-hand, talking and laughing, felt like I was being physically tortured, taking me back to moments I would never have again in my life.

When I was out, I didn't want to see anyone I knew. I didn't want anyone to see me, and I was on full alert that there were triggers all around me.

Every small thing I did felt like a heart-wrenching reminder that she was gone.

It was no one's job to fix me or try to make me feel better. That was impossible. However, when it looked like I was able to function, I know it made other people feel better within themselves. It took some of their own pain, fear and worry away and allowed them to breathe a little deeper.

Many nights, as I lay in bed feeling broken and numb, Rob and I would meet each other in that space. We didn't need to say anything. We both knew nothing could be said. We'd just hold each other, cry, and hopefully fall asleep to be taken away from our pain just for a little while.

After many conversations between us, Rob encouraged me to start the diploma in which I was enrolled, in Sydney. I reluctantly agreed to go for the first week—two days. Not because I wanted to, because I had no idea what the hell I wanted or needed, so I just agreed to try.

I will never forget that first day—just six weeks after losing Ella. I got in the car, drove two hours to Sydney by myself, and before I knew it, I was there. I don't remember the drive. I was on autopilot. I got out of the car, my stomach churning as I made my way into the classroom. Knowing nobody, I sat behind a desk and tried to be present. An impossible task.

As the teacher spoke, I questioned why I was there. I couldn't focus or concentrate, but I stayed. I looked around, watching everyone listening attentively, and wondered how I was going to do this. At morning tea, a lady spoke to me. I didn't really want anyone to speak to me, but she was kind and I felt partially comfortable telling her briefly about losing Ella, through the tears, when she asked if I had children. The ice was broken. I made it through the first day and went back for another day.

I continued to drive to Sydney two days a week for the next eighteen months, studying Kinesiology and Mind Body Medicine. That place and those people became a huge part of my healing journey. I didn't realise it at first, but I was exactly where I needed to be. This was part of my medicine.

It wasn't easy. I had trouble remembering and retaining information. I put additional pressure on myself to try even harder, as I didn't understand what was happening and why. Later, I learnt trauma's effect on the brain can be strongly associated with memory function. That made so much sense.

When it came time to practice what we'd learnt and do full healing balances on one another, my emotions were raw. I was processing and healing, little by little. Some days I would cry all the way home. Some days I would cry all the way there. But there was something inside me that kept me going. It was like a tiny little flame that was smouldering deep within the depths of my core. I felt like Ella was keeping this light on for me—just enough for me to continue to put one foot in front of the other and not give up.

I need to do this for Ella. I just have to keep going, I kept thinking. *Her life must have a purpose. This cannot have happened without there being a reason.*

Something inside me believed I could, and I did. In my mind, there was no other option for me. This was exactly what I was meant to be doing. This was my purpose and Ella was leading the way.

When I look back at the events that unfolded in the lead up to Ella leaving this world, there are so many things that happened that are too aligned not to believe there was a higher source at play. There is no other explanation that can explain this for me or help me to understand.

We were blessed to have found out about an amazing charity organisation after we lost Ella, SIDS & Kids, who provided counselling and support to families who had lost children to sudden infant death syndrome and those whose children had passed away unexpectedly. The one-on-one counselling I received through them became a lifeline for me. My counsellor had an amazing way of connecting me with my emotions and my body. She taught me so much that I was able to bring forward into my own life and the lives of others over the years. Another incredible human that Ella brought into my life.

One of the modalities they used as part of the therapy was Sand Play, a type of expressive therapy where you create scenes in a large sand tray that act as a reflection of your life through feeling. At first, I thought it was a little silly and was unsure how it could help, but I was always open to new opportunities to process and express how I was feeling. It was powerful. Through this creative expression, often nonverbally, I was able to process some of my trauma, develop a strong sense of self-awareness and recognise patterns in my life that were no longer serving me.

SIDS & Kids gave our family, including my boys, the most amazing support. They taught us the differences between the grieving process of men and women—which I'm sure at times saved our marriage. This was such an important part of our journey through grief, which I believe is never-ending. So many couples don't survive this rollercoaster ride together, which is so heartbreaking when they are already going through so much pain.

Now called Red Nose, they still provide an invaluable service to families who are dealt the cruel hand of having a child taken away too soon. They rely heavily on donations, so I decided they would be our chosen charity to raise money for in memory of Ella.

I had a beautiful friend who lost her three-year-old son tragically when my boys were around the same age, many years ago. It was such a struggle for me to even comprehend how she could survive the pain and I always felt such compassion and love towards her. When I lost Ella, she was there. At my door. Weeding my garden with some of my other beautiful friends. Sitting with me in my grief. She knew this pain only too well.

One day I walked out onto my front verandah after she'd been there to find a beautiful big white stone angel sitting by my door. It touched my heart deeply as I looked at her and thought to myself, never did I ever think I would be feeling this same pain that you've had to go through, and continue to go through, every day of your life as a grieving mum.

Part of me still didn't believe I was. It was a strange feeling. Surreal, but so real at the same time.

I also realised around that time that I'd never participated in any of the group sessions offered by SIDS & Kids. At that stage of my journey through grief, my healing was something I felt I had to do on my own, or when the going got tough, with the assistance and guidance of my counsellor.

I had adopted a belief system that I had to take care of myself and do the work that had to be done—alone. During those times, I drew on an inner strength and resilience that I had built up over my life. It felt very powerful at times, but it often made it hard for me to let those who loved me the most in, to let them sit with me in my deepest, darkest moments of pain.

> **I realised whenever I felt like I didn't want to go through with a process that was there to help me heal, it was my fear of the unknown holding me back, which usually presented as anxiety, and sometimes panic. This was my signal that it was exactly what I needed to do.**

I made a commitment to myself to feel the fear and do it anyway, and continued to slowly move forward, learning more and more about myself as I healed and transformed slowly through my grief and past wounds.

I discovered that as I started to process and heal, what I often thought was the part of me that required the most focus and attention was just the surface layer of what was really going on. The wounds were deep. Moments of profound realisation started to take place. I was seeing things that had happened throughout my life in a very different way as I allowed the unravelling and the deep inward journey to continue.

≈

Reflection Song: I Will Carry You—Selah

13

My Boys

*'Being brave isn't the absence of fear.
Being brave is having that fear and finding
a way through it.'*

Bear Grylls

My fear of loss was strong. Tim was still not well. Losing his little sister sent him plummeting into a place he didn't always know how to get out of. One night, as I lay next to him to hug him, he said, 'I just want to go and get her, Mum.'

'I know, Tim, I know. So do I.'

How do I take my children's pain away?

I can't. It's impossible.

I had to do what I wanted everyone to do for me. Meet him there, in that space, and just 'be there with him'.

This wasn't hard for me to do, but it was scary. There were times Tim's feelings were too heavy and dark for him to bear. I was so blessed that he was always able to come to me when that happened, although in the pit of my stomach I was terrified.

Not only was this triggering the loss of Ella and my desperate need to ensure I never had to lose a child again, but it also triggered a wound from my teenage years—a wound forever etched in my soul.

When I was fifteen years old, my boyfriend, my first love, committed suicide. The first death I fully experienced, the shock and devastation were overwhelming. I couldn't understand it. It broke me.

As children, we weren't allowed to go to funerals. I guess this was seen as a way of protecting us from pain and grief, but really, it just felt like it made things more confusing.

You can't protect someone from the grief they feel.

It didn't help when we were faced with death head-on later in life, with no idea how to work through the emotions and feelings.

So, the first funeral I ever attended was when I was fifteen years old. I remember walking towards the coffin at the front of the huge Catholic church to place a yellow rose on it. Trying to navigate my way through overwhelming grief and sadness, with what felt like very little resources to draw on, was so daunting. Lost in confusion and unanswered questions, the direction of my life had been changed forever. It was hard, really hard.

I was heartbroken and in deep grief. My parents were scared for my wellbeing and my life—which they had every right to be—because there were plenty of times I didn't want to be in this world as I tried to navigate my way through that intense time of my life.

I remember regularly not going to school. I'd go to the medicine cabinet, looking to see what I could take to remove the pain for good, wondering if there was enough to end it all, but never being able to go through with it. I didn't want to put the people I loved through the shocking pain I was experiencing, but I was hurting so badly and had no idea what else to do.

I was now reliving this in a different context, as the parent, sitting with my heartbroken sixteen-year-old son, in deep pain and grief, telling me he didn't want to be here. I wasn't sure how much more my heart could take, but I knew exactly how he felt. We were both breaking inside.

Tim is witty, funny, very kind-hearted and generous, has a smart mouth and can finish my sentences a lot of the time. We often know what each other is thinking and about to say before we say it. It can be hilarious, and at other times, not funny at all! I'm sure if you have, or know, one of these children, you know exactly what I mean. This is a kid who was born cheeky, cute, and seemed to be able to make everyone laugh and he knew it, loving every bit of attention he could round up. But he is sensitive too, extremely sensitive, with a huge heart. As I sat with my beautiful, broken boy, I didn't know what to do.

My eldest son, Sam, is soft, gentle, caring, kind-hearted, smart, and sensitive. He would do anything for anyone (a beautiful trait to have, as long as you can give enough back to yourself). He feels and thinks deeply and has an amazing ability to be fully present with people. We have some beautiful, honest conversations together. I feel he has a very old soul, full of wisdom.

Even though their beautiful qualities cross over, my boys are so, so, different. It is often hard to believe they have the same parents. Tim likes to remind us that he is the only child who was planned. Sam and Ella were both beautiful surprises, coming into our lives at exactly the right time. However, we did plan to have Tim, so to him, he likes to think that makes him 'extra special', and he lets everyone know.

Sam shows his grief differently, more outwardly, not holding it in as tightly as Tim, but I could see he was also breaking inside. We spent many nights side-by-side, talking and crying as we held each other, trying to make some sort of sense out of our new family structure with the huge, unwelcome hole in it. Sam went back to continue his studies. I look back on this now and wonder how he managed to do that. I guess we have more in common than I realised. I admire them both so much, each for their individuality, and for the strength they drew from within themselves in the darkest of times, even when they probably were not even aware that they were doing so.

A lot of my energy was directed towards Tim during those months, due to his health issues and my fear of losing him. My fear was strong. In my mind, Sam seemed to be coping a little better on the outside. Maybe that's because he can express his emotions a little more openly, which helps to process them. Even so, I could feel his deep heartache and pain.

We were all just trying to sail our own lifeboats without sinking.

Sam was someone Ella looked up to and loved to have fun with. They took snapchats on his phone and he was there to help her with her homework and reading if I wasn't available (that is, if her patience would allow him to). She loved to play games with him, especially interactive games on the Wii machine, like Guitar Hero and Let's Dance. Sometimes I'd find her hanging out with him in his bedroom, often during times when his girlfriend was around. They loved spending time together.

Tim and Ella were so much alike—with strong personalities that often clashed, neither liking to give up. It wasn't unusual for me to have to sit Tim at a different table to eat dinner so he'd stop stirring her up, just trying to get any sort of reaction out of her he could, which he thought was hilarious. Besides the frustration this dynamic brought to me at times, they had lots of fun together building Lego®, watching movies, swimming in the pool, riding scooters and jumping on the trampoline. They loved each other dearly. They fed off each other's energy. On rare occasions, I'd see them sitting together, Tim listening to her read or him reading to her. It was beautiful.

Both boys had precious, unique relationships with their little sister. She cherished them dearly. And now they were both heartbroken.

All I could do was be a safe, reliable, loving place for them to land.

Reflection Song: Satellite—Ben Abraham

14

Grief

'Don't allow others to rush you through your grief. You have a lifetime to heal and it's a lifelong journey. Travel at your own speed.'
　　　　　　　　　　　　　The Grief Toolbox

None of us knew Ella was only here for a short time. I believe in my heart she was only ever meant to be on this earth for ten years and nine months, and that she'd been sent as a gift to our family to teach us all many lessons as she travelled through this dimension. We were never meant to know how long she was here for.

What would we have done if we knew? Wrapped her up in cotton wool?

What sort of life would that have been for her?

Ella had an amazing life full of extraordinary experiences and so many incredible holidays. She was a cheerleader—a flyer! You know, the one they throw in the air. She had beautiful friends and made friends everywhere we went.

I choose to look at Ella's life in this light and I choose to live life in her honour, learning the lessons she was sent to teach me as I travel through my personal life journey on this planet, however long that may be.

I had no control or choice of when I had to say goodbye to my little girl and I can never change that, but I do have the choice of how I want to show up in the world and live my life from this point forward.

This is my choice, and this is where my power lies.

We all have a choice.

However, this is not something that always came easy for me.

Rob was now the parent of two boys who had lost their sister. He knows their pain—it's all too familiar. I worried about him. Why did he have to be brought into this family to experience more pain and suffering?

I know this was his choice, and there were obviously lessons he had to learn through this too, but it hurt me deep inside to know he was hurting. I felt his pain along with my own. I felt everyone's pain—it was exhausting.

I am so grateful though. Grateful he was present with me, even when he was not, even when I was not emotionally available to him but could be physically present. It's hard to balance.

Physical presence in these times can be enough (sometimes), just to know someone is there. However, this was not enough for either of us. We needed each other to lean on for emotional support, to hold and cry on and be in that space together.

Grief is complicated and hard to understand.

We worked through it the best way we could. Rob was there when he could be, but work took him away often. He had a company to run and a family to support. Work was also his way of coping, as it had been for a long time. It was a distraction. We all tried to find ways to distract ourselves, because the pain was just too much to bear most days. He recognised that, but it was all he knew.

We continued to get support through SIDS & Kids, and were reminded that people process grief in many ways, and that the ways we grieve are in no way gender specific. Often, men are seen as the protectors and providers and women as carers and nurturers. However, we all start our personal grief journey at a different place, even when we are grieving for the same person. This is based on our connection and attachment to the person, what our past experiences have been and what resources we have to draw on from within ourselves.

We learnt about two types of grief: Intuitive Grief and Instrumental grief.

This information is based on an article written by Red Nose Grief and Loss on Moving Forward: Do Men and Women Grieve Differently? The full text is available online at Red Nose Grief and Loss Services – www.rednosegriefandloss.org.au.

I feel it is important to share this information, as it may help you to have a better understanding of what people are going through in their darkest moments of grief, and how this can be so different for each person. I've done my best to put it into my own words, based on my personal experience.

If you grieve intuitively, you'll experience and adapt to grief on an emotional (affective) or feeling level. You probably find it easier to express what you're feeling, and there's likely to be a lot of crying, perhaps even shouting. Emotional and physical support are important for you. You might find yourself obsessed with thoughts of your child, and the nagging 'what ifs' and 'if onlys' can monopolise your thought processes.

Grieving can take longer for the intuitive griever, and often appears more intense than for the instrumental griever. It's not hard to imagine how this can create issues in relationships if the intuitive griever feels the instrumental griever doesn't care as much. Everyone is unique, so women don't all grieve one way, and men another, but women are more likely to grieve intuitively, in verbal and emotionally expressive ways, sharing their grief with others. Traditionally, men have been offered fewer outlets for expression of grief, socially or at work, so support groups can be helpful. Some also find creating a project or activity in memory of their child a positive outlet.

If you experience instrumental grief, you'll find doing something, planning and managing activities may be your more natural expression of pain. The benefit here is that doing something can help to provide a form of stability in a world that no longer makes sense for you.

Your activity is future oriented, not looking back as much, so not getting as caught up in the 'what ifs' as the intuitive griever. While the majority of men may be instrumental grievers, due partly to their role causing them to rationalise their loss in relation to the wider family, women can be instrumental grievers too.

Instrumental grievers won't tend to be as publicly open and obvious in their grief, preferring to grieve privately. For many, this is due to the ability to compartmentalise their grief, allowing them to 'get on with life' by allocating certain times or situations for grieving.

Understand that not finding time to express your grief, because you feel your form of expression doesn't meet the expectations of others, or you think you need to be strong or keep going with 'normality', even though normality as you knew it has forever changed, just tucks your grief away to be dealt with later. This can cause problems on all levels—emotional, physical, spiritual and psychological.

And here's the kicker—you might start off grieving intuitively, but as life's demands, the expectations of others and possibly your feelings of needing to protect others pull at you, your emotions get pushed down and you become more instrumental in your expression of grief.

However you and the ones you share your life with grieve, intuitively or instrumentally, it's important to work to support each other, and know that one approach is not better or more superior to another. If you grieve intuitively but your partner grieves instrumentally, as time goes on, your partner may feel as though they are failing you, as your grief continues to be openly expressed while they appear to be coping and needing less. The key is to be aware of each other's natural grieving style and support each other with as much love and sensitivity as you can, accepting when the tanks are empty and all you can do is be there.

Rob and I found that we each fell into both categories, intuitive and instrumental, at various times. I know Rob often felt helpless in his efforts to connect with me and guide me out of my darkest days. We talked to each other often about how we were feeling, which we knew was important for both of us. Internally, however, we were both trying to process our pain in our own ways, which was different for both of us at different times on different days. It was something that didn't always align and wasn't easy for us to understand in the moment, especially when we were sitting in separate places within ourselves.

It was definitely not something we could predict in any way, but I knew at the end of each day I would be held in those strong, loving arms that were there to love and protect me in any way they could, not trying to repair the unfixable, but holding me close to cry more tears that had often been held in for too long. No words were needed as we lay in our grief, questioning why this was now our life and wondering if the pain would ever end.

Grief is unpredictable. I learnt from the early days of sitting in it that planning things in advance didn't always work, as I never knew how I was going to feel on any given day.

Often, it would be the smallest things that would trigger the deepest, darkest of moments.

Like finding a little note Ella had written that I'd never seen before or had forgotten about. A song. Seeing her friends reach milestones that I knew we would never have together. A Mother's Day card. A random comment from someone. A photo. Christmas. Anniversaries. Birthdays. Holidays. Family dinners that no longer resembled my family. A Facebook memory.

Pretty much all of life's moments that were happening around me, while the rest of the world functioned like nothing had changed, were potential triggers.

We do the best we can with what we know at the time, in the moment, processing our own feelings and emotions and learning what we can along the way, opening ourselves up to allow new opportunities for personal growth and healing to enter our lives when we feel we have the capacity and resources to do so. That is all we can do.

Reflection Song: Clouds—Before You Exit

15

New Beginnings for Some

*'We all die. The goal is not to live forever.
The goal is to create something that will.'*
Chuck Palahniuk

October 2014

Before we lost Ella, we'd organised a trip to Thailand with friends. I no longer wanted to go, but Rob thought it would be good for us. I couldn't bear the thought of leaving the boys, so we asked them to go with us. Sam didn't want to miss his studies, so stayed with his dad, while Tim decided to go with us for part of the trip.

This was such a relief for me, as I was so worried about him. I'm not sure I could have gone without him. It was another distraction, for all of us. He had some fun and it was nice to see him smiling again in little bursts, although his pain, along with mine, was bubbling constantly below the surface.

During that time, my sister Kylie was due to have her baby. My only sister, sixteen months younger than me. A week after Ella left us, Kylie had a scheduled ultrasound to find out the sex of her baby. She turned up at my doorstep, as she'd done every day since June 7, 2014, and looked at me with tears in her eyes.

'It's a girl.'

I knew in my heart it would be. We cried. I told her it was ok, this was how it was meant to be. Her baby would be such a gift to our family. I wanted to be there as her support person during labour. I had no idea how I'd cope with that emotionally, but it was something I really wanted to do. She'd been such an amazing support for me and was so heartbroken herself, while still trying to bring up her own children, Tayah and Jye, through all their grief. It was so hard to watch their little hearts breaking. So, as I headed to Thailand, I prayed each day that she didn't go into labour until I got home.

Then I got a Skype call, and there she was—my new little baby niece, Scarlett—born just minutes prior. Overwhelmed with emotion, tears streamed down my face. I just wanted to be there with her. I needed to hold her in my arms. I wanted to go home—immediately!

The feeling of being so far away tore me apart.

Distance
I could not be there to hold on to your hand,
But my heart was there, you understand.
To know you were in pain tore my heart in two,
But I knew you could do this, with an angel watching over you.

I know she was there with you all the way,
In that very same room she was born on her day.
And she held your hand for me when I was not there,
You knew she was with you, in this moment I could not share.

> And into the world came a precious gift,
> To make us feel love and give us a lift.
> To open our hearts so they can give love once more,
> To a precious baby girl who has touched our hearts' core.
>
> Kim Cameron

I know there's a reason I wasn't there for her birth, and I believe it would have been overwhelming for me to be in that room.

How is it that life can be taken away from us in the blink of an eye, and yet the world continues to revolve as new life is brought in each day. This process of life and death that is never really talked about happens all around us, every day, and it's not until we are hit in the face with it that we remember we are all guests here on this planet. Nothing is permanent.

How do any of us know we're not ticking time bombs, just waiting for our moment in this lifetime to cease? We don't. A lot of us take for granted that we'll just be given the gift of waking up tomorrow. While I continually strive to bring positivity and hope into my life, it's impossible to do this without being honest, realistic, and speaking my truth.

If I could not acknowledge the fact that I could die at any moment of any day, I could never feel the gratitude I have for life itself.

While this may sound a little morbid, and something not everyone wants to think about, this recognition is what gives life such amazing value.

With this deep knowing in my soul, and the fact I'd been given the gift of continuing to live my life (for however long that may be), a fire ignited inside me that helped me to continue to move forward, taking one step at a time, one foot in front of the other. I made the decision in honour of my beautiful baby girl to make the most of whatever time I had left and help as many people as I could along the way.

What did this mean for me?

It meant I had to work on myself. That I must commit to 'doing the work'. Healing myself from the inside out, so in turn, I could hold space and guide others to do the same—even when it's hard, when it hurts, when it's scary and uncomfortable, and especially in the times when I want to run away from it all.

I decided I was going in—into myself with love, into my wounded places that were calling for my attention. This was not negotiable for me.

I know my wounds will always be part of who I am and the hurt will never go away, but I want to be able to navigate through it to a place where it no longer holds me with such an intense grip. I want to learn how to be the container to hold it, instead of feeling like I am being so contained. Finding healing in my trauma, I want to swim in its awareness with presence and love. This feels like the greatest lesson that I am here to learn as I come to know myself as life itself.

Reflection Song: The Last Day on Earth—Kate Miller-Heidke

16

My First Retreat

'Listen to Silence. It has so much to say.'
Rumi

As part of my diploma, I was required to attend a retreat, run over three days by some of the course facilitators and counsellors. Having never been on a retreat, I felt excited and a little anxious. It was very early days. I was still processing a lot of my grief, and every other feeling that comes with that—guilt, anger, regret, despair—just to name a few.

Some days were better than others. Some days were pure hell.

I'd be camping with one of my classmates for the weekend. We packed the car and drove into the mountains, set up our tent and got ready for whatever was coming, which we had no idea about. A huge step into the unknown. A beautiful lesson of trusting and surrendering. Leaving my family was difficult, but I knew I had to do this for me.

Over the next few days, we were taken through several processes to help us connect with ourselves and drop deeper into our own bodies. This would assist to process the feelings and emotions that lay within us as the layers unravelled.

One of the first exercises was a trust exercise. Obviously, it was important to establish trust within the group before we could move into deeper processes. The first one wasn't too bad. Blindfolded, we were led by a partner around the bush. I had to put my full trust in the other person that they wouldn't lead me into danger but would keep me safe—a strange feeling! I discovered I was more comfortable guiding someone than being guided, which was a good insight.

The next part of the trust exercises was to allow yourself to be held by the group. A person steps into the centre of the circle and closes their eyes as they start to move their body a little—keeping their feet stationary—relying on everyone in the circle to support them. Their body drifts from side to side, until eventually they are moving in all directions with ease. The circle then places their arms underneath the person as they are lifted off the ground, suspended in the air, supported by everyone. I imagine it feels a little like being rocked in a cradle.

I felt a little unsettled. I was able to hold the others—just—although it was a hard task for me emotionally. When it came time for me to step into the circle, I wanted to run. My nervous system was activated and my fight/flight response had been triggered. I left the circle. It was too overwhelming to allow those people to hold me. I just couldn't do it.

A facilitator came to check in with me. I couldn't understand why it was so hard for me to even fathom the thought of allowing this beautiful group of people, who I was sure had nothing but love and compassion for me, to hold me in their arms. Aware that I was still stuck in a trauma response, my sympathetic nervous system being on high alert, the facilitator supported me and encouraged me to come back into the circle—which I did.

I wasn't ready to let them hold and support me, but I'd stay and hold space for them.

Processing had begun.

I sat with myself and asked *why is it I cannot allow others to support me?*

> **Being curious about myself and my feelings**
> **keeps me on a path of self-discovery**
> **and inquiry.**
> **I learn so much more about myself from**
> **this space.**

I have always been so independent, doing things on my own, getting things done. Some say I come across as confident and strong. I realised I was scared—scared I would break open even further if I allowed those people to hold me. Allowing myself to be nurtured felt foreign. I wasn't sure I knew what to do with that.

As the retreat went on, I moved through each process with commitment and a depth of sincerity I hadn't felt before. With a deepening connection as I walked through nature in silence, I started to reconnect with myself. I slowed down. I breathed. I allowed myself to feel, and to express how I felt. I softened as I sank gently into myself. My nervous system started to settle slightly.

Heading home after the three days, I was changed. I was not the same person. I felt this was just the beginning for me and it strengthened my commitment to continue on this path.

I will continue to grow and honour the gift I have been given to stay on this earth.

Being Brave

The journey deep within
Takes a brave, committed soul.
The journey deep within

Can seem like a dark, deep hole.
A hole within my core
Searching for the light.
A place that feels so raw
Often pushed out of sight.
Just waiting for a chance
For me to take that step.
Just waiting for that dance
For my heart to reconnect.
Kim Cameron

Reflection Song: Trust—Alexia Chellun

17

Processing in Circles

'There is no greater gift you can give or receive than to honour your calling. It's why you were born. And how you become most truly alive.'
Oprah Winfrey

I met so many amazing people as my studies continued. The processes and sessions we worked through as part of our training allowed me to feel deeply and move through some of my trauma and grief.

Powerful, it gave me full insight into just how deep this kind of work could take not just me, but those around me I am working with and those witnessing the changes taking place within me. Something happens deep inside me when I'm surrounded by people who are brave enough to be vulnerable and stand in their truth. It's a contagious energy that is so beautiful and graceful it leaves me yearning for more.

I knew this was my calling. There was such a deep sense of knowing that I didn't have to question it. The only time I did was when fear and doubt crept in to block my path, causing me to second guess myself—another sign for me to dig deeper, get more curious and investigate where it came from so I could move through to the other side of those feelings and emotions.

There was no other way for me anymore. I couldn't just walk around it. My self-awareness became stronger each time I took another step within. There was no going back. No more pushing anything back down into my body. I had to go through the fear to see what was on the other side, allowing whatever came up to complete its cycle fully as I became aware of patterns that no longer served me in any way—patterns that had been passed down to me through generations and learnt behaviours that I had adopted to keep safe and feel loved.

As painful as it was at times, being able to tap into my body to locate areas that were holding onto stress and emotions as I worked through them, one by one, until I felt my body letting go, just a little, was such a blessing. Sometimes it was exhausting. On rare occasions, I questioned if I wanted to put myself through it. There was a part of me that believed the deep pain in my heart would never go away, yet I also believed I must do whatever I could to live my best life possible, for myself and for Ella. Feeling a little lighter, even if only for a small window of time, was enough for me to know I must keep going.

One of my teachers was running a retreat outside of college and invited students to attend. A brilliant teacher with an incredible energy, I could listen to him for hours as he portrayed his experiences and life stories with such passion, which is such a gift to the world. Also a photographer, he knew my story, so one day I asked if he could work on a photo I had of Rob and Ella to see if we could get it a little clearer.

Rob's favourite photo from our wedding, it features him holding Ella as they swing around the dance floor together, just seventeen months before she left this world. She laughed and giggled, throwing her beautiful blonde curls back in the air. The raw emotion and connection in that one picture is priceless. It is a moment in time that

Rob treasures and a memory that brings such warmth to my heart—a picture of pure, joyful love.

I also asked if Rob could attend the retreat with me, and he said yes. Rob was very interested and said he'd like to, although he was nervous and a little anxious, not knowing what to expect, which was totally understandable.

Even now, I sometimes wonder, had I known what to expect when I embarked on the journey of looking within myself with great depth, would I have decided not to open the lid of that box at all. Then I feel into my body and check in with my higher self and am reminded very quickly that it was always going to be this way.

I realised that when I feel any form of anxiety or apprehension, this is the signal for me to stop and tune into my heart, as my mind is usually trying to hijack the situation and control the outcome in some way as to what decision I am to make. It comes up with some pretty incredible stories that often hold no value or truth.

I was learning to recognise such moments and the self-sabotage that was being created as the anxiety attempted to pull me down and keep me stuck in a very low vibration.

Each time I had this awareness, I was able to reconnect to myself by slowing everything down, finding a quiet place (preferably in nature), breathing deeply and allowing my body to have the space it needed to realign and remember.

In this space there is no doubt, only a deep sense of peace and unshakeable inner knowing.

We all have access to this in every moment of our lives. We just need to slow down, as this is never available to us when our lives and minds are too busy.

My heart always knows what is best for me. It calls me away from my fear and supports me with love as it signals me to step through it.

Stepping out of my comfort zone to do this work is where I have experienced the greatest growth. When I have chosen courage over comfort and allowed myself to be vulnerable enough to let go and show up as my authentic self my deepest healings have taken place. Some of the stories I kept hearing on repeat that I had to acknowledge and work with were:

> I could have done something to save Ella.
> I should have known.
> I could have been a better mother.
> I should have been more present.

These were some of the thoughts that tortured my mind!

Even with the awareness that I had, those stories still dragged me down into a space that I sometimes sat in for longer than I wanted to when I could not find the courage to face them. When that happened, I would take myself away to be in the quiet darkness of a corner of my bedroom or sit beside my daughter's grave.

Some days, I felt it all and it was so overwhelming. I relived every moment of the night in the hospital repeatedly in my head. The flashbacks would come and go. I tormented myself trying to remember the last conversation Ella and I had.

Other days, I felt nothing. Being disconnected from all emotion seemed the way to go, a survival mechanism that felt like it gave me enough of a break to go on for another day. The choice to get out of bed and function was agony. Yet each day, as time passed, I kept putting one foot in front of the other. Each day, I tried to remind myself that every little thing I did was an achievement. It was like stepping over an imaginary line in the sand and discovering what I thought was my limit, never was. That line in the sand could be swept away by the incoming tide and moved to higher ground at any time, and I knew I had to make the choice to continue to follow it.

Then there was another feeling inside me—a determination to just do whatever I needed to do to move forward, driving me on auto pilot as I continued on the path I was paving for myself.

This was to be Rob's first experience attending a retreat and giving himself the time and space to connect within. We were both giving ourselves a gift. Space to feel. To process. To heal. Together, yet alone.

I felt grateful and blessed that Rob was open to going. Our journey together had dealt us the unimaginable. Being open to new ways and opportunities to heal was the only way for us to continue to grow and stay connected as a couple through our individual hurt and pain.

We both come from families who have experienced tragedy and grief, as most families do in some way or another, and our parents and grandparents come from an era where there was not the support that is available to us. The common belief back then was that you just had to 'get on with it' or 'soldier on', pushing feelings and emotions down in whatever way possible to survive. Feelings were not often talked about, shared, discussed or acknowledged, and there often wasn't the time, space or support to do so.

This is what had been passed down through generations and influenced our development and the conditioning within us both, yet we knew we wanted something different, to change these patterns and be able to grow and feel depth within ourselves and together. We wanted to show our children that the cycle did not need to continue in the same way it had for hundreds, maybe thousands of years.

Rob and I were both harbouring wounds, not just from losing our precious Ella but from years of grief we'd both been carrying around. Together, and individually, we'd created patterns in our lives that seemed to help us cope and keep going in those moments when all we really wanted to do was stop and fall apart.

We'd both experienced broken relationships and heartache, tragedy and grief. We were now trying to bring our lived experiences together to create a connection between us stronger than we'd experienced before with anyone, and we both wanted something much deeper and very different to what we were experiencing. We were hurting and it felt like a very heavy burden.

Rob and I knew in our hearts we had something very special and there were many reasons we'd been brought together in this lifetime. Relationships are not always easy, and we were aware we had to continue to work on ourselves for our connection with each other to strengthen and grow stronger with time. We could not connect with each other on a deep level if we were not connected to ourselves. This could not occur unless we were both prepared to look within ourselves.

Like most couples, life had created different triggers within us that caused us to react defensively at times. We became unavailable to ourselves and to each other, thinking we were protecting ourselves from more pain, yet often doing the exact opposite—dancing around issues that needed to be addressed and understood, particularly our broken hearts, shattered dreams and a future that would never be the way we'd envisioned. We were both doing the best we could with what we knew and the life we now had, while trying to be open to learning new ways of healing.

I learnt that when I am triggered by something someone says or does, it is because it's cutting into a wound I am already holding within me that is calling for my attention to the healed.

If it wasn't, then it wouldn't hurt in the first place. It wouldn't trigger a reaction or response and I would not feel wounded or attacked. In my moment of reactivity, be that silently within or an outward expression, I have a beautiful opportunity for growth if I choose to see it in that light.

It's only when I take the time to sit with myself and work through where this has come from that I often realise it has nothing at all to do with what the other person has said. It's usually related to something that has been pushed down into my body for years that I haven't given enough attention or time to. Left unresolved, it is still having some sort of control over my life.

So, what will happen if I never stop to look at this?

The pattern will continue, and my life will never be any different. My reactions will still be the same and I will never take full responsibility for myself.

Sometimes it seems so much easier to blame those around us when we feel upset or hurt, rather than to take full responsibility for ourselves and our own emotions.

So, I sat in it. Giving myself the space to sit fully in it, I worked backwards—taking responsibility for myself each step of the way as I made conscious decisions not to continue carrying the pain any further through my life or pass it down to the next generation.

I asked myself, *what will happen if I don't?*

What if I allow this cycle to continue and don't do the work on myself?

What will happen if it does keep getting passed on, if no one takes responsibility for making this change—who will ever break the cycle?

I wonder if maybe this is part of my purpose?

Healing the wounds of my past, of past generations, for the future of my children and their children.

Acknowledging this felt like an enormous responsibility. However, I knew that my body was already carting this around anyway on a cellular level, so it was not going to be anything new.

So off we went to my second retreat, and Rob's first. He was the only male apart from the facilitator (David). I knew some of the other women from college, but I was meeting most of them for the first time. One of my other teachers, Tracey, was also there to assist David and participate. What a beautiful group of people. We all took food to share and spent the next three days processing, healing, creating, journalling, meditating, resting and being with ourselves. It was a very emotional and reflective time.

One song that was played that we spent time reflecting with over the weekend was a version of *Mad World* sung by Michael Andrews and Gary Jules. It reminded me of the power music and the spoken word has on us, evoking a lot of emotion for me as I lay in silence, listening to each word, tears rolling down my cheeks.

Rob said he was glad he went, even though some of the activities were a little confronting for him as he connected deeply to the pain he was carrying. This was so for everyone at different times as we stepped outside our safe comfort zones to grow a little.

Rob is a very sensitive, caring man, one of the reasons I love him so much. Everyone was so supportive. The connection created between us all felt sacred and irreplaceable.

Leaving that weekend, I knew this was something that my soul desired to do—bring people together to connect to themselves on a deep level and process whatever they were carrying in their physical and emotional bodies that created imbalance within. There are so many people hurting who need this time and space, to feel the connection to themselves and to others in a non-threatening environment where they feel they don't have to hide or be someone they are not.

I knew in my heart that one day, this is what I would be doing.

Reflection Song: Mad World—Michael Andrews, Gary Jules

18
Ella's Walk

*'Real generosity toward the future lies in giving
all to the present.'*
Albert Camus

September 2015

SIDS & Kids were a pivotal part of our healing process. The support and counselling we received has not only been my personal saviour, but also one for many other members of Ella's extended family. I had a strong calling to give back. I also wanted to help Ella's friends find some peace and continue to keep her memory alive. It broke my heart to see them hurting. Ella's death changed their lives in so many ways, some they weren't even aware of yet. Losing a friend at the age of ten is something that shapes you as a child and as you continue to grow into an adult.

It changes so many things.
How you see the world.
Trying to make sense of death.
Questioning why.
Feeling emotions you may have never felt before.
How do children manage this when adults struggle so much?
I organised a team to be part of the annual 'Walk Australia' charity walk, an event held in different parts of Australia. Our entry fees went to Walk Australia, whose

chosen charity was the John Hunter Hospital—where Ella was operated on and where she passed away. We personally raised additional money to go to SIDS & Kids, to give back to this incredible organisation that relies heavily on donations to assist them to continue to help as many families as they could who experienced the unexpected and inconceivable loss of a baby or child.

The walk was held on 13th September 2015, the day after Ella's 12th Birthday. Our Team, 'Team Ella' all wore blue—Ella's favourite colour. Over 150 people walked as part of Team Ella that day. It was simply beautiful, and I know in my heart that Ella was there walking with us. I had caps made with 'Team Ella' embroidered on them by a local embroiderer who did them for us at cost price. The generosity of people touched my heart.

Looking around, all I could see was a sea of blue. Surreal, and a little overwhelming, knowing we were all there together because Ella had to leave us.

We gathered for lunch after our walk, raffles were held, and we raised $15,000 from that day alone. As we had the biggest walking team, the organisers asked me to speak at the end of the walk, in front of hundreds of people, so we could let everyone know why we were walking. I didn't hesitate, as I knew how important it was to get the word out about the amazing work SIDS & Kids were doing for the community and to bring awareness to people about Arterial Venous Malformations (AVMs, the cause of Ella's death).

AVMs are a tangled mesh of abnormal blood vessels that form accidentally prior to birth and directly connect arteries and veins to the brain, brainstem or spinal cord, which disrupts normal blood flow and oxygen circulation. For Ella, it occurred deep in her brain.

AVMs occur in approximately three in every 10,000 people. They appear rarely in several generations of the same family, and are not believed to be genetic. They are also said to be more common in men. Bleeding from an AVM most often occurs between the ages of ten and thirty, and less than 10% of AVMs that have haemorrhage as the first symptom are fatal.

The most common symptoms of AVM (according to the Australian Brain Foundation) are:
- Sudden and severe headache, which may be localized or general, or resemble migraine headache in some cases.
- Vomiting occurring with headache.
- Vision changes including decreased, double or blurred vision.
- Seizures (fits).
- Muscle weakness in any part of the body.
- Decreased sensation in any part of the body.
- Sleepiness, lethargy, disorientation, irritability.
- Stiff neck.

Our little girl was one of the very few unlucky children to be born with what was, for her, a fatal condition.

Standing on the stage in front of all those people, my heart felt like it was going to beat out of my chest. My throat tight, I held back the tears as I told our story. There was silence. I can only imagine what the other parents there listening felt, their hearts heavy, finding it hard to comprehend this was even a possibility that could happen to anyone, let alone a child.

I never share our story to upset others or for sympathy or pity—that is the last thing I would ever want.

I tell our story in memory of Ella in the hope that people never take life for granted.

I told our story then, as I do today, in the hope that people would hold their children a little tighter, lie with them a little longer and live a life without regret, remembering that every single moment in this life is a gift.

My purpose behind sharing is also that it may give someone else a sense of hope and the strength to draw on their own resilience to try and find meaning in life when tragedy strikes, and to understand the power of the human spirit when faced with extreme adversity.

I never thought in my worst nightmare my child's death would be part of our lives, part of our story, making us into the people we have been forced to become as each day goes by.

None of us are protected from the unknown, unseen pain that life may throw our way at any moment.

You can make as many plans as you want to, but in the end, it's often about letting go of all those plans, dealing with the heartache and making a conscious decision about the life you want to create from this point forward.

Letting go of those plans is hard, especially when they are ripped away from you with such force, which feels like nothing other than pure cruelty. It is in those moments that you realise how little control you have.

I had to find a way to accept that this was our new life and we had to live it the best way we possibly could as we had been given that opportunity, Ella hadn't.

We continued to raise money for SIDS & Kids as the years went by, holding a Gala Ball called 'A Night Under the Stars in Memory of Ella' on 23rd July 2016. A huge event, I managed to organise it in just four months, with the help of family and friends. 240 tickets went on sale and sold out in less than a week. It was crazy. We did so much work getting donations and prizes together for an incredible night of raffles and auctions. Holidays and accommodation, a beautiful hand-built cubbyhouse, vouchers, bottles of wine and personalised candles—were donated, along with elegant table decorations made from fresh blue orchids, balloons, live music—we had it all. It was such a beautiful, amazing night that I will never forget. I could feel Ella was there with us.

As I stood in front of those people to talk about Ella, some of whom were my closest friends and family, the emotions were overwhelming and got the better of me. I looked around to see everyone there in the one room—in honour of my daughter. I could have fallen apart right then on that stage. My heart was breaking. My throat was aching. I had so much gratitude for each person present, and most of all for my beautiful daughter who had touched the hearts of everyone in front of me, some of whom she never even knew. Scanning the room, I realised how much love and support we were surrounded by. It was incredible.

Wow, Ella, you are the brightest star in the sky. Your essence has entered the lives of so many. Your departure has touched more people than we were even aware of, and you have left a gift so powerful it will continue to change lives long after we come to join you.

We raised over $50,000 that night. I couldn't believe it. It was so awe-inspiring and amazing to see what we were all capable of when we came together, our hearts open wide. Ella wove her magic once again, bringing people together, just as she always wanted it to be, for one amazing cause.

As successful as the night was, I knew in my heart it would be a one-off event. As much as everyone encouraged me to do it all again, I was exhausted. It had been an emotional roller coaster and consumed so much of my time and energy. It was worth every second, but it was time for me to slow down.

It was time for me to move forward and remember Ella in a different way. I knew I had to continue to look inwards, not outwards, to strengthen my connection with my beautiful girl.

And so the journey of looking from the inside out continued.

Reflection Song: A Sky Full of Stars—Coldplay

19

I'm Scared

'Something will grow from all you are going through. And it will be You.'
Author Unknown

The fear of losing those close to me remained strong. I'd do anything within my capability to keep my boys safe. The thought of losing someone I loved was excruciating. I couldn't imagine this being worse than what I'd already experienced and was going through, but I guess it could be if anything happened to my two boys.

Post-traumatic stress is real. I relived the night we lost Ella over and over in my head. Seeing her lying unconscious in emergency. Rushing for MRI scans, surrounded by crash carts. Watching her being hastily wheeled into the operating theatre. Walking out and leaving her in the hands of people I'd never met—trusting them to try and save her life.

The feeling of having no control over anything was crippling.

I couldn't get the image of her little white coffin being lowered into the ground out of my mind. Wanting to stop what was happening, while thinking at the same time *this can't be real!*

Part 2 – I'm Scared

The fear doesn't go away. I feel these moments will haunt me forever.

The sound of an ambulance siren sends shivers down my spine and tears to my eyes if they pass me on the road. I imagine her lying inside, unconscious, fighting for her life.

My nightmare started to relive itself as Tim's health declined. He came to me to tell me he was not ok—which I already knew. I also knew exactly what that meant.

Tim was in Year 10 when we lost Ella. He did not go back to school. He started to work for Rob as a trade assistant, but with the physical and emotional symptoms he was experiencing, it was just too hard for him to manage every day in an industry that required such long hours. Tim was admitted to a private hospital for depression and anxiety. He felt that was where he needed to be. Each day I sat with him, not always knowing what to say or do, just being there so he knew how much he was loved.

I was so scared. I didn't know what else to do to help him. All I could do was be by his side and pray that the professionals could provide him with tools to process some of his grief and pain. He was at such a vulnerable age. He punished himself harshly, telling me what a terrible brother he was to Ella (which could not be further from the truth).

He rang me one morning from the hospital, after a few weeks of trialling different medications, to tell me he wasn't taking his medication anymore as he felt it was making him feel worse and he wanted to get off it all. I rang the nurse to find out what was going on, telling her I felt like I needed to take him home and I wasn't happy with all the medication changes he'd had in such a short period of time. I felt he was being overmedicated. The nurse was old school, so I was surprised when she told me she thought it a good idea. She also told me we could get a second opinion.

When I asked her how, she said I'd have to check Tim out of the hospital and check him back in under a different psychiatrist. How ridiculous. I told her there was very little chance of me getting Tim back to that hospital once I took him home.

This had been Tim's second stay there. His first was a few months earlier, resulting in him pretty much checking himself out earlier than planned. It had been a struggle for him and frightening for me. He so desperately wanted some reprieve from the hurt he was feeling, but I couldn't really see how him being in the hospital was helping. They provided information sessions and group sittings each day that Tim never attended, so he spent most of his time in his room alone anyway. I thought he would be better off at home with us, surrounded by people who loved him.

I trusted my gut, got in the car and drove to the hospital. Walking into his room, I wrapped my arms around him and told him to pack his bags. He looked at me in disbelief.

'Yes, mate, we're going home.'

We had to meet with his psychiatrist before leaving. Tim was anxious, worried the doctor would not agree with our decision and that I might lose my cool with him. He did not like conflict. I assured him I would not, but that I would be firm and assertive and advocate for him, as he wasn't feeling strong enough to do that for himself. I told the doctor our plan—that we were taking Tim home to gradually wean him off his medication, as it was making him feel worse, because that was what he had indicated to me that he wanted.

The doctor told me he thought we were making the wrong decision. That's ok, he was entitled to an opinion.

So were we!

I was listening to what Tim wanted in that moment, just as I had listened to what he had wanted when he asked to go back to the hospital. It was confusing for him. He was hurting. I had to trust what felt right.

We never saw a psychiatrist again and we did manage to get Tim off the heavy medication he'd been put on in the hospital. It's a long journey that continues and will continue for years to come. This is part of what makes him who he is now. It's part of his life. Navigating through the world of grief is hard. It hurts and can be debilitating; however, we cannot change anything that has happened. All we can do is manage it in the best way we can as individuals, surrounding ourselves and each other with love and support.

All I can do as his mum is be there for him to remind him how loved he is, especially when the days are too hard and he doesn't want to be here anymore because the pain seems unbearable and he cannot find a way out of that space.

I am forever grateful that he always comes to me when he's in a dark place. I have an unbreakable bond with both my boys that I treasure. I have always told them no matter what sort of trouble they are in, or how they are feeling, they can come to me or call me at any time, without any fear or judgement.

Witnessing him in so much pain broke my heart. Knowing I couldn't take any of it away was even harder. No parent wants to see their child hurting, especially when there is no possible way you can make that pain go away.

It hurts. Bad.

≈

Reflection Song: One Day At a Time—Jeremy Voltz

Our Life with Ella

12th September 2003. Ella was born. Sam, Tim, Craig (Ella's dad) & Ella.

Our Happy Baby. Age 1.

Ella. Age 3.

Ella, Kim, Sam & Tim. Enjoying life on holidays in Foster. 2007.

Our Little Dancer

Sam, Ella & Tim (left to right).

Ella & Tim.

Sam, Kim, Ella & Tim.

Ella Loved Animals

20

It's Time

'She believed she could, so she did.'
Author Unknown

August 2015

I continued to study until I received my first Kinesiology qualification. Officially allowed to practice in my own clinic, I had the innate knowing this was what I was meant to be doing.

My determination and fire kicked in as I worked towards creating something positive in my life where I could help others. Knowing the power of this modality, having experienced it firsthand many times, I was excited to share it with the world.

When asked to describe a Kinesiology session, people often don't know what to say. Usually, it's something like, 'You just have to go yourself, be open and feel what happens for you.'

Every experience is unique. I have personally experienced so many different emotions and feelings in all the sessions I've had over the years—a sense of lightness, release, balance, deep connection, realisation, understanding, awareness, and peace, just to name a few.

The definition of Kinesiology on the Australian Kinesiology Association's website says 'Kinesiology encompasses holistic health disciplines which use the gentle art of muscle monitoring to access information about a person's well-being. It combines Western techniques and Eastern wisdom to promote physical, emotional, mental, and spiritual health. Kinesiology identifies the elements which inhibit the body's natural internal energies and accesses the life enhancing potential within the individual.' (https://aka.asn.au/what-is-kinesiology/)

I cleared out the office at the front of our house and began to set up my clinic space. I bought a second-hand massage table to work on, designed my own website, ordered business cards and went to Ikea to buy a new desk and storage unit.

I had everything I needed—except my confidence.

The fear stepped in. It was loud, that voice in my head that said, 'Who are you kidding? Who is going to want to come and see you? You're a grieving mother. You must still be in so much pain, it wouldn't be fair for us to come to you with our problems.'

This will never work. What if I put my energy into setting this up and follow my heart and I fail?

There it was.

What if I fail?

Thus came the stories that played on repeat, over and over in my mind. I worked with my counsellor to help with this old story that seemed to keep arising in my life—*what if I fail?*

I was taken back to a place in my life when I felt like I did fail. I tried so hard and failed in front of everyone. In my eyes, I screwed up big time, performing on stage as a musician in Canberra when I was fifteen years old, something I'd worked towards for years. I practiced for hours, usually on a complicated movie theme or original piece of music my teacher composed for me to perform, until perfection was reached, or until my sister was yelling from her bedroom that she'd heard enough, or it was too loud.

I liked to play loud. The louder the better at times. The pieces I played were usually intensely moving, emotional and dramatic and just didn't sound the same plugged into a set of headphones. Music moved me. It helped me to process my own feelings and emotions and I just loved to play.

Well, most of the time! The nuns at my Catholic girls' high school I attended used to put anyone they knew could play well on a roster to play the morning assembly hymn, while everyone sang. I didn't always love that!

The year I got through the local and regional levels and was off to perform at state level in Canberra was a dream come true for me. I was my teacher's 'prize student'. It was an amazing feeling to have reached that level and to feel like I'd made other people proud, as well as myself. All my hard work was paying off.

I walked on stage to an auditorium filled with people. My family had travelled long distances to see and hear me play. My mum, a talented dressmaker, had made me a beautiful dress, as she did each year for my performances. This was my chance to shine.

I got about halfway through my piece, to a part that was relatively simple compared to the rest of the song, and I literally had a mental blank. As my fingers glided over the keys of the electronic Yamaha triple keyboard, my feet dancing across the foot pedals in a crazy choreographed way, I couldn't remember the next note I had to play. My heart skipped a beat as I went into panic mode. I'd been practicing and playing that piece of music for months, but suddenly I couldn't remember a simple frigging note! I botched it, playing a few wrong notes. I told myself not to stop, just keep playing. The feeling in my chest was heavy and my stomach was churning as I held back the tears.

In my eyes, I had failed.

Although I managed to get through to the end without any more mistakes, it was not good enough for me. I was devastated. I was disappointed in myself and felt I had disappointed my teacher and my family.

So, in the moment of weighing up if I was ready to start my new business, that was part of the story that played over in my mind. *What if I fail?*

And it felt very real...

> **It is incredible how our past experiences can shape our future ones when we have not given our feelings and emotions the time and space to complete their full cycles, storing them in our bodies until they are triggered again, often by completely unrelated circumstance.**

That voice in my head was my enemy and my best friend. It gave me a lot of excuses, but also a lot of determination. As I spent time working through those feelings and old stories, I was able to process what was really going on for me and understand that this story no longer served any purpose in my life. It was time to let that old story go. It was not true and did not bring anything of value into my life.

One day I woke up and said to myself *this is the day*. I don't know where it came from, but it was there and it had power, love, strength and the determination I needed, teamed with a deep knowing that this was exactly what had to be done, today!

I got out of bed and walked into Ella's bedroom, sat on her bed for a while, closed my eyes and felt her presence. We talked.

I received clarification that now was the perfect time, I just had to trust.

I walked out, launched my website, posted on social media and set my days that I would be working in my new clinic, called E K Kinesiology (E K for Ella Kate and for Ella and Kim).

You'll never guess what happened—people actually started to come and see me as a practitioner in my own clinic!

Crazy, right?

There were still moments I doubted my own ability and questioned if I knew enough, which I knew was coming from my overthinking mind, not my heart, but I was doing it and it felt so beautiful.

I hadn't worked with other people in a professional capacity since losing Ella, apart from helping Rob a little with his business when he needed me to while I was studying. For the first time in over a year I'd be working with people face-to-face.

It was a little daunting, to say the least.

I was apprehensive about having people come into our home, and slightly curious about how having a lot of different energy there would impact us all, but I knew I was in no position to commit to renting a space or working outside of my home. Home was my safe space. It was also where I felt Ella was closest to me and that was where I had to be for now, even though I knew in my heart she'd be with me no matter where I was working from.

It was exciting, and as I witnessed people having positive, life-changing experiences, I started to realise that I did have something to offer this world. I knew Ella was working alongside me and often felt her presence as an energetic tingle through my legs. As my intuition grew stronger, I was able to listen and trust myself more, without giving my mind permission to take over and make me second guess myself.

It took a while to find a healthy balance of how many people I could see in one day. I did tire myself out some days, which started to have a negative impact on my own energy. Feeling zapped at the end of a day was a strong signal that something had to change.

Once I realised what was happening, I adjusted my workload, ensured I was clearing my clinic space and myself of energy after each client and became more mindful of keeping my work in that space only, not taking it into my home.

I continued to study until I'd completed my Diploma in Kinesiology and Mind Body Medicine. I am forever grateful for the love and support I received from the College of Complimentary Medicine staff and teachers where I studied, and for my beautiful classmates and friends who held me with compassion and as much understanding as I could possibly ask for over the time we spent together. Many of these people saved me in so many ways. From hugs and conversations when I thought I could speak to no one, to Kinesiology balances that helped me to move forward, sometimes in the smallest of ways.

I look back now and have no idea how I managed to get through that time in my life. I remember having emotional breakdowns at exam times, wondering if I could complete what I had started and often feeling stupid because of my inability to retain information, constantly doubting my own abilities.

But I just kept going—and I finished what I had started to create—a beautiful new purpose in my life.

Reflection Song: Prisoners & Guards—Aisha Badru

21

Spirit of Woman

'Life is a matter of choices, and every choice you make, makes you.'
John C Maxwell

November 2015

Accepting Sunshine
Each moment in time has a purpose,
Each moment in time I have a choice.
At my darkest of dark times - it is so hard to find light,
Yet I continue to search - I will not give up,
Even though some days that's all I want to do.
I put on my mask and smile,
Until one day I can smile no more.
The truth is revealed – I crumble,
The depth of my sadness has reached its limit - and now it overflows.
I allow myself time - to sit in my truth - to feel it all,
To give it time and space to be as it is – in whatever form it takes.
And then out of nowhere – through the darkness,

Your little ray of sunshine somehow finds its way back into my heart and soul.
I'm reminded of the gifts you have given me,
How blessed I have been to have you grow inside of me.
I am reminded of the amazing and beautiful times we spent together,
Now memories - ingrained in my heart forever.
I have stopped asking why - as these are answers I will never have,
But one thing I do know - is that you changed my life in ways I could never imagine.
You were sent to put me on my path,
And now I understand
Why you had to leave.

          Kim Cameron

I wrote this just before I was called to go deeply within myself again. Powerful healing takes place when you immerse yourself in the space of a retreat. The indescribable feelings and experiences had been so profound and life-changing for me. I wanted more. There aren't many other places where I feel safe to process my own pain and emotions in safety, with support from those who have the ability and skills to hold space with love and understanding, without judgement and without feeling like they need to fix anything.

In that space, I trust and allow my body to do the work. It knows exactly what I need, in the right place, at the right time.

The body has the ability to make itself sick, and equally, to heal itself. This was something I strongly believed in. I knew on a deep level that I wanted to share that with others, and the only way to be able to do that was to keep 'doing the work' and have these transformational experiences for myself that I wanted to be able to support others through.

Powerful shifts were taking place within the opportunities I was being guided to as I continued down this path. So off I went again on my third retreat—a six-day women's retreat at Mette's Institute in Kin Kin, Queensland (also known as High Spirits Retreat). It was just over seventeen months since I'd lost Ella. I'd been working through a lot, yet it was all still extremely painful and raw. My heart was broken. And yet, as I evolved, I was slowly creating a very different version of me that I hadn't known existed.

My body was holding on to so much that I wanted to process and let go of to create space to live the best possible life I could for myself in honour of Ella. This felt like my reason for living, the reason I'd been left on this earth. Ella had so many lessons to teach me and I was determined to do my very best to learn as many as I possibly could in the time I had here.

Rob dropped me at the airport for my flight to Brisbane. As we embraced, tears flowed. He held me tight as I questioned why I was leaving the safety of my family to embark on an unknown journey. I felt the fear of entering an unfamiliar space where I knew no one.

Sitting alone in the waiting lounge at the airport, asking myself *what I am doing here,* I heard Ella's words ring in my ear, 'Mum, just do it!'

Ok, ok, I'm listening. I am going.

The retreat recommended there be no contact with the outside world during the six days. I understand why, as it's so easy to be pulled away from yourself when you're going deep within, particularly after speaking with others who may not understand why you're doing what you're doing. Hearing other people's thoughts and opinions that may influence you in some way, or simply knowing what's going on in the outside world, can easily do this and be detrimental to the reason you entered the retreat environment in the first place. So, while it's hard, it is also part of the healing journey.

A retreat is a sacred space where you get to discover your true self. Even though there are other people present who you may connect with in different ways, and people who will trigger you for many reasons—they are also there to connect with themselves on a deeper level and heal in their own way.

There can often be a lot of fear from those around you who love you, including your partner, spouse, children and family. I mean to say, they have no idea what is happening for you on retreat or who the person that comes back to them will be.

Will you be the same? I highly doubt it. Landing in Brisbane, I made my way to the bus terminal. I saw a lady in the distance, wearing a beautiful hat, looking just as lost as I was. Out of everyone there, something told me we were heading to the same destination in the Queensland Hinterland. I trusted my instincts and approached her to ask. She was, of course!

We introduced ourselves and shared our trepidation of the unknown. Her name was Katie. We were soon picked up by a private bus and sat together for the two-hour ride to our new home for the next week. We talked about our careers and life in general, then the bombshell question came.

'Do you have any children?'

I hadn't quite worked out how to answer that question, no matter how many times it was asked. I mean, the answer is yes, I do have children, but how do I speak the truth without upsetting others or getting upset myself? Sometimes this feels unsettling for me. Sometimes it doesn't. I wanted to tell Katie the truth, so I did. Of course, it was devastating to her as a mother. However, if I was to spend the next week with her, and many other women, I would have to be able to share my truth for me to be able to give myself the best opportunity to continue to heal. I could not protect others.

There were over twenty women attending the retreat. Katie and I were allocated to share a room with two other ladies, which was nice, because we felt like we already knew each other a little. The location was beautiful, high in the mountains. I felt like I could breathe there.

As we traversed through the week we laughed, cried, shouted, danced, sang and moved. We ate well and cleansed our bodies and minds. We were still and silent. We went within ourselves, looking deeper than ever before. We experienced the incredible power of KaHuna massage, a massage that originated in the South Pacific and was used during Rites of Passage for transformation and healing. KaHuna massage provides a holistic approach to healing by balancing the body and mind in the physical, emotional, and spiritual dimensions. It has so many benefits, including the feeling of deep calmness, peace, and relaxation along with its ability to re-energise and rejuvenate the body.

I'd already been using KaHuna massage as part of my healing as I'd been allowing myself to peel back the layers. Every experience is different, but I always find it's a great way to unlock stuck emotions and energy in the body as it shifts blockages and creates a deeper connection to myself.

My KaHuna massage during the retreat was so beautiful and emotionally raw as I opened my heart fully and allowed some of the pain and suffering to be released from my body. Tears fell freely. When I got off the table I felt so much lighter and more peaceful and my breathing was deep and gentle.

Each time I allow myself to go to the vulnerable places within to heal, I am creating space within my body for energy to flow and for change to take place.

It is truly magical.

Reflection Song: Like a Lake—Sara Groves

22

KaHuna Homecoming

*'Not everyone will understand your journey.
That's alright. You are here to live your life.
Not to make everyone understand.'*
　　　　　　　　　　Author Unknown

I felt like a different person! It was a challenge to go back out into the world after the depth I had experienced over the past six days. We were transported back to the airport. The noise around me was overwhelming, and I wasn't even in the airport yet!

It's amazing to think how alive my senses became after just one week of removing all distractions and noise. I started to hear everything on a whole new level. I was listening to myself and my body. Food tasted different and my sense of smell was really switched on—I was literally smelling the roses.

It made me question the world and how and why I, and others I witnessed around me, tended to get so consumed 'doing' and keeping busy, thinking we were 'living'. Now so much more aware of the imbalance within and around me, I stopped to ask myself *how do I want to live out my days on this earth?*

How do I want to feel a decade from now?
How do I want to feel today, tomorrow, next week?

What do I need to continue to do now to create a life where I feel connected and can thrive?

What do I need to let go of and change?

One of the biggest problems I've experienced and witnessed is that we always think we have more time. This way of thinking is naive and unrealistic as there are no guarantees in life. That's something I've had to learn the hard way and one of the greatest gifts I have been given. It's so easy to get caught on the treadmill!

As I started to see more clearly, with an open heart and mind, I was realising that I'd not been living in a way that aligned with my soul at all. I'd been chasing my tail, surviving for years—setting goals, then pushing myself to achieve them, so I could set more. And while I do believe it's important to have goals and something meaningful to work towards, I knew some of my goals were not as important as I initially thought or made them out to be. I wanted to create more balance in my life.

Hindsight is a beautiful thing.

I wish I'd known years ago, when my children were babies and growing so quickly, what I was finally learning.

I wished I hadn't thought I'd have them forever.

I wished I'd left the dirty dishes in the sink and spent more time playing and feeling the joy.

I wished I hadn't worried so much about having everything done before I gave myself permission to rest and relax.

I wished I could get some of that time back so I could slow down and make time to really assess and feel into if I had to go to work every day to make more money, to buy more things, or if I could have spent more time doing what I loved—being a mum.

I wished I'd known how to breathe deeper, how to let go of the small stuff and not worry about things I never had any control over anyway, knowing that worry was never going to change the outcome of anything, apart from preventing me from feeling at peace.

I wished I'd slowed down enough to be able to tap into the knowing that has always been inside me so I could trust myself fully and listen to my heart.

But sadly, these wishes can never come true for the life I have already lived. It was not my time then to know this. I did the best I could with what I knew in those moments.

> **My time is now, and this is what I must trust.**
> **I cannot change the past. I can only live in the present moment with more awareness and connection to myself and those around me and make the changes I want to bring into my life today.**

I was understanding more and more the importance of bodywork in healing. I found that when I was working in my clinic, it was so easy for some people to get stuck in their heads, telling their 'story', often handing their own power over to others by blaming them for the things that were happening in their lives, not taking responsibility for themselves. They believed the feelings they were experiencing were real, when often they were based on their own evaluation and interpretation of the emotions they would have initially felt.

I had been in that place myself so many times.

Emotions are based on real time data, sparked by sensations in the body. This was the connection we were trying to re-establish. Once people were able to connect with the visceral messages coming from deep within the body, rather than from their intellectual minds, they began to develop emotional awareness. This then started to reduce their reactivity to life, as they were no longer being as triggered by their feelings but deeply connecting to their own emotions.

> **Emotions are a wise language within us all, always trying to give us useful information to stay regulated, resilient, and show up as our best selves.**

I could see how KaHuna massage could assist greatly and work as an incredible infusion with Holistic Kinesiology and Mind Body Medicine. I was so passionate about this healing modality that I put it on my 'bucket list' to learn. It was a big commitment to myself as I knew this was a deep journey, comprising seven levels of training, with each level having specific processes to encourage deeper healing and self-awareness.

So, I decided I would start training. It was important for me to find something that would work with the body in a way that felt right for me. Working with meridians, the energetic pathways that run through the body and can store different emotions within them, felt like it would work well with the wisdom of the Traditional Chinese Medicine concepts I had studied as part of my Mind Body Medicine Diploma. I'd start training in Lomi Lomi Massage, with the dream of working towards training in KaHuna massage one day.

So much physical pain is caused in the body by emotions that have never been processed or released. Needing to be stored somewhere, they sit within our bodies creating blockages and imbalances. There are so many reasons for this, one of them being that a large percentage of people are not even aware of the different types of alternative therapies available to assist with this. There can also be a lot of fear around going into parts of ourselves that we are not familiar with. Fear of the unknown.

I personally found that stepping into the spaces that provided me with the support and time that I needed to process my emotions was essential for me to not be weighed down by my past experiences. It is the only way I have been able to move forward and find some peace in my life after experiencing devastating loss.

> **I have found it is the best of you that comes into being after you face your greatest challenges. Challenges expand us, helping us to see where we need to continue to place our focus and energy, while illuminating the places where we have grown.**

Many want a 'quick fix', that is, they want their pain alleviated immediately. Who wouldn't? Western Medicine is quick to prescribe medication and pain killers, but these can mask the root cause of what is really going on underneath the symptoms, physically and emotionally. I know this to be true because I've experienced this firsthand on many occasions.

Often, blockages and imbalances in the body have been developing for years. By the time they present on the outside of the body as physical pain, there can be a lot more going on underneath of which we are not even aware. It takes time and commitment to look inside yourself and not everyone is ready to make this type of commitment to themselves, and that's ok. It can be scary, yet I believe it can be a wonderful way to prevent further illness down the track.

As I slowly weaned myself off the medication that had been prescribed to me in an attempt to lessen the pain I was feeling and be able to survive each day after I lost Ella, I was able to continue to process emotions as I felt them arising instead of having them supressed within me.

I now had more tools, support, and awareness to be able to navigate my way through this in a more healthy and conscious way that aligned with me.

> **We don't just get sick for no reason.**
> **When we take the time to stop and really**
> **tune in and listen to our own bodies, we**
> **start to understand that symptoms are**
> **not enemies to be destroyed, but sacred**
> **messengers who are there to encourage us**
> **to take better care of ourselves.**

Reflection Song: Big Love, Small Moments—JJ Heller

23

How Do We Connect Again?

*'The walls we build around us to keep sadness
out also keeps out the joy.'*
                                    Jim Rohn

Marriages that have sustained the loss of a child through death experience the same valleys and peaks as any other marriage, just in a more exaggerated form. Whether they become better or worse, the one sure thing is that the marriage will never be the same as it was before the child's death.

This was true for us, and we continued to work with our counsellor to understand the different ways in which we were grieving, the different issues we had to deal with, personal resources we were able to draw on and our different personalities and pasts.

It was hard for me to allow joy and happiness back into my life. It almost felt wrong, like if I felt a tiny inkling of it, I shut it down and went back into my pain body. How could I possibly feel joy again? I wanted to. Well, I think I wanted to. I wanted to be able to have fun and laugh again, but part of me felt so broken inside and guilty for even wanting those things back in my life.

Yet I knew I needed to for my boys, for Rob, for my family and for Ella. Most of all, I needed to do it for me.

So, I made a conscious choice that I would focus on allowing joy back into my life. I didn't want to continue feeling the heaviness that weighed on my shoulders daily, or the seriousness that had embedded itself into my heart, making it hard for me to continue on the path I had chosen.

For three years following Ella's death, after having happiness snatched away from me in a heartbeat, processing the emotions and feelings of denial, guilt, sadness, regret and deep grief, along with the times when numbness took over, happiness didn't always feel like something I wanted to invite in, or even felt at times was possible.

Losing Ella is part of me; it contributes to what makes me, and is making me the person I am and the person I am becoming every day. I never want it to completely disappear—not that it ever could. I tell myself, if feeling this pain is the price I have to pay for loving her so deeply, then it's worth it. A part of me is gone forever and this is what I am now left with to process and recover from. It felt heavy.

I know this is part of what I've been put on this earth to work through. And while it never seems justifiable that children have to leave this world before their parents, in what is called the 'unnatural order of death', it is a part of life that we have no control over.

I am committed to this part of my journey and determined to continue to do what I feel is necessary for me, to heal in whatever way I am drawn to.

I am ok with this.

But what was not ok was for me was to stop enjoying life. I knew this was having an impact on my relationships with others, my marriage and myself. I felt sure Ella would not be happy if she saw me not living life to the fullest. My most beautiful memories of her were seeing the gorgeous smile on her face, her blue eyes beaming and her little cheeks glowing with colour as she threw her head back and laughed. What a picture of pure joy that was.

That is what I needed to hold onto.

I was once told by a psychic medium that it had been hard for Ella to get through and connect with me as my pain was so deep and intense. I didn't ever want her to feel that pain I'd been carrying, and I certainly didn't want to block her from being able to connect with me.

After developing such intense pain in my hips that it was difficult for me to walk comfortably some days, I was called to have another KaHuna massage. What showed up through the massage was that I'd been energetically carrying Ella, along with all my emotional pain, on my hips. I could feel it. It was crippling me, holding me back—physically not allowing me to move forward.

Emotionally, hip problems can relate to taking on too much responsibility and carrying others, feeling burdened, undervalued, unacknowledged, unsupported, and unappreciated, along with holding on to feelings of frustration and guilt. I could resonate with most of that.

After an intense two-hour massage and a lot of emotional release, I could move again—the shift was incredible. I felt Ella in the room that day. She kept coming and going, just to make sure I was letting go.

That night I had the most amazing experience.

Every night since I had lost Ella, I would talk to her when I went to bed, asking her to come and lie with me so I could hold her close, just like she used to when she snuck into my bed in the middle of the night. I just wanted to be able to hold her—one more time. Although I knew in my heart one more time would never be enough, I so desperately wanted to see her again.

And I did.

That night as I was sleeping, she came to me through a visitation dream. I could see her so clearly. She was sitting on the end of my bed. I picked her up and carried her out to the lounge where we sat and cuddled each other. It was the most beautiful experience I've ever had. We weren't sad, we were just there, our arms wrapped around each other in an irreplaceable moment in time. We didn't speak, although I felt like she was talking to me through her heart, telling me she'd been waiting to get this close, and it was time for me to let go of some of the heavy pain I'd been carrying.

It was so different from a dream. This felt real.

When I woke, I experienced an overwhelming feeling of peace and contentment. As much as I wanted that moment back, a gentle smile came over my face and I realised once again the power of letting go, along with the power my body had to hold onto my pain.

Thank you, Ella.

I felt so much lighter and started to feel a little ray of light creeping back in through the cracks of my heart. I knew my heart could not fully open to give and receive love with the heaviness I'd been carrying, and I knew I was the only one who could change that. Often, I wasn't exactly sure how to do that, but I was determined to try whatever was sent my way that aligned. Doing the inner work could only enhance my connection with myself. The connections I formed with others could never be any deeper than that. Honouring what I needed and having faith was the first step towards this.

**I believe it is possible to transform every area of our lives if we choose to do so, and that is no one else's responsibility but our own.
I take full responsibility.**

Reflection Song: Your Love Walks With Me—Claire Bowditch

24

Listen Carefully

*'If you don't heal from what hurt you, you'll
bleed on people who never cut you.'*
Author Unknown

Healing is a continual, constant process. There is no final destination, as much as some days I would like to think there is. At this stage of my life, I am just working towards being the most authentic version of myself I can be, day by day, hour by hour, minute by minute.

Once I started the journey inwards it was hard to look back. I just kept allowing myself to feel it all, to acknowledge what was happening in my body and mind and be open enough, and at times brave enough, to step forward into the unknown. I had to listen so carefully. Tuning in more and more to the sensations in my body, becoming aware of my own aches and pains and what emotions they related to, I began to get a clear understanding of what my body was holding on to and how it was trying to get my attention.

In my past, before I had an awareness of the connection between the mind and the body, I was quick to take medications to suppress physical pain—never addressing the underlying issues of why the pain was there in the first place. At that time of my life I didn't know any different. I know now that my body will always tell me what it needs.

Developing this emotional intelligence helped me to live in the present moment where I could stay connected, assess my own needs, manage my reactivity, and make conscious decisions. This way of living means I must put myself first, listen to what it is I really need and slow everything down. I have found that most people I work with (including my past self) are very good at creating distractions in life, keeping extremely busy or putting all their energy into helping other people so they can tell themselves the story that they don't have time to look after themselves. I personally recognise this pattern as a form of self-sabotage. The question I must ask is this—if I don't have the time and energy to look after myself, who is going to do it for me? This is no one else's responsibility, except mine.

> **When we blame others, we avoid looking at ourselves and our own behaviour. The more we lash out and protest about the unfairness of it all, the more stuck in the problem we become.**

This is a cycle I never want to be part of again. Taking responsibility for our own healing means we can no longer blame negative experiences and use them as an excuse to behave in a way that could hurt others while continuing to inflict pain on ourselves.

Believe me, I know it can be a scary concept to delve into that abyss of the unknown that resides within. How long have you been stuffing toxic feelings and emotions down into the sacred vessel you call your body—all the unexpressed anger, resentment, guilt, sadness, worthlessness, and the inability to say what you really want out of fear of rejection or judgement.

Using substances and participating in activities we think will make us feel better, by sending short bursts of endorphins to our brains, through drugs and medications, food, caffeine, alcohol, sex, pornography, distracting ourselves by shopping, gaming, binge watching television or finding other ways to numb ourselves out. So many distractions!

How many times have you inflicted your own pain on others by reacting harshly because something they said triggered something you've been holding onto from your past?

When I am fully honest with myself, I can say I know I have. I believe even the most enlightened people would say the same, because these are the challenges we have to navigate in life to learn the lessons we were sent here to learn, to evolve.

Hurt people, hurt people. This is true. This is how pain patterns get passed on from generation to generation. People who hurt people, consciously or unconsciously, are always carrying hurt from being wounded in some way. Note that this is not an excuse for bad behaviour. Breaking the chain and turning your hurt into compassion for yourself and others can be a long road. It can also be a beautiful one that will change your life forever and bring you back into alignment with the magnificent person you were put on this planet to be.

This is usually not something that will happen from reading a few self-help books or having one session with a therapist. It is a commitment to your own personal growth, for life. Each time you're triggered by something someone else says, it is a message that there is an unhealed part of you calling out for your attention and love. Be kind to yourself. Our relationships are our greatest teachers.

Think about past relationships where you were hurt in some way (this could be a friendship, romantic connection or family). You might have walked away from that relationship eventually, but what happened to the hurt? Was it ever really processed, or was it just pushed down into your body until the next unlucky person came along who said something that triggered that same wound again? Most times they are the ones who cop the brunt of years of pain, suffering and pent-up feelings and emotions.

Another great example is the relationship you had with your parents (I know, that is a whole other book), but how many of us lived our lives trying to meet our parents' expectations? That's what children learn to do, in the hope of receiving what we were all craving—love, acceptance and belonging. We learnt at a very early age what sort of response we would receive from our parents by exhibiting certain types of behaviour and often adapted our behaviour to get that response. It's human nature.

I learnt from an incredibly young age that being 'well behaved' and not complaining a lot meant most adults were very loving and affectionate towards me. I was accepted and loved by my parents, family and teachers. So, I adapted to be the 'good girl' as much as I possibly could. At school, at home, out in public—that was how I learnt to get love—behave well. Behaving badly, or having emotional outbursts, usually meant I was reprimanded in some way, sent to my room, or grounded. And if it happened out in public and I was chastised for behaviour that didn't meet social expectations, it often accompanied feelings of shame, guilt and feeling bad about myself because I had disappointed others.

This type of behaviour often results in repressing emotions until they build up to a point where they can no longer be held in. That started in my late teenage years when I rebelled. There were a few reasons for that:

One—I was hurting, so it didn't matter to me if my behaviour was hurting others. Remember, hurt people, hurt people.

Two—I'd had enough of being that person who was always so well behaved, yet I didn't have the skills or supports in place to know how to change it.

So, I ran away from home when I was sixteen, trying to find who I was by following others. Lost and grieving, I was looking for love in all the wrong places, through the love I thought I could get from other people.

There have been a lot of studies and research done in this area and I am no expert, but I know what I feel, and I know what I see, and how other people tell me they feel when they come to sit with me. The amount of work I've done with clients, and continue to do, working with their Inner Child, is testament to this.

Working with our Inner Child, or what I like to call our Original Self, helps us consciously change how we relate to ourselves. When we can connect with this part of us, it often helps us to begin to care more deeply and bond with ourselves as we start to experience critical realisations from our upbringing that have influenced our subconscious programming early in our lives.

The sooner we recognise these adaptive behaviours we've carried into adulthood in some way or another (and very often passed down to our own children), the sooner we can start to investigate and discover who we really are. That is, our true nature, who we were before we were conditioned and made decisions to alter our unique selves to feel loved.

It is important you have access to the tools and support you feel you may need to navigate through this time in your life, should it arise, even if it's a friend who can really listen to you. For a lot of people this doesn't happen until they reach their middle years of life, age forty-plus, then people start asking if they're having a midlife crisis, which I find quite interesting. If a midlife crisis is about turning inwards to find out who you really are as a person, before you were moulded into a version of you that you created around the expectations of others so you would be loved, then so be it.

I was having a midlife crisis.

However, I think that losing a child at this age can also contribute to this.

Part of this journey for me has brought up so many fears, and I know in my heart and soul the only way through the fear is to face it head-on. I spent way too many years avoiding conflict and pushing things under the rug to keep the peace.

I often imagine a road sign pointing in two different directions, telling me I have a choice of which way to go. I can stay stuck in the feeling of fear or anxiety when it arises or look at it as an opportunity to keep moving forward, stepping out of my past conditioning and creating new energy and patterns within myself.

Once the fear has subsided, I often wonder why I had to torture myself for so long. Change for me has always been on the other side of fear. There is something deep inside me that feels it is my purpose to feel and process it all. Moving through the fear can often be confronting, confusing, painful and scary, but what comes after is such an incredible shift that it's impossible for life to ever be the same again.

There is so much power and potential within us all, yet so many of us walk around with our masks on, scared to even look what's behind it. Dare yourself to take it off. It can be so freeing.

Everything that has happened in my life has led me to where I am today. Every challenge, heartache, loss, disagreement, and connection I have ever made, all the love I have experienced, the gratitude and joy, the pain, and the sorrow. All these things are part of what makes me who I am, and in each moment, I know I have done the best I can with what I knew at that time of my life.

But now I know more. Now I feel more, trust more. I can listen more deeply to that voice within me, my own wisdom. Now I can do things differently. I can respond instead of reacting. I can have more awareness of what is happening for me, and for other people around me. I can come from a place of deep compassion and love and can choose not to be part of drama. I can free my mind from unnecessary thoughts that keep me stuck in old patterns and cycles. I can choose every day how I want to live and create my life according to that.

I can love myself—and that's where it all changes. Self-love is a matter of self-worth, and I am worthy. My own self-awareness can only strengthen this love.

When we start to release our grip on how we think our lives should be, we create space for our lives to flow freely. Attachment is control and blocks our appreciation for the amazing things we already have in front of us. Let go.

Reflection Song: The Art of Letting Go—Fia

25

Moving Forward

*'Holding on is believing that there is only a past.
Letting go is knowing there is a future.'*
Daphne Rose Kingma

May 2017

So many lessons kept coming my way—all guiding me back to being authentic and showing up in the world as my true self. My eldest son Sam, at twenty-two, talked to me about wanting to get to know me better. He felt he didn't know me for who I really was, other than being his mum. I love that he is open to having deeper connections and conversations with people and is not afraid to talk about his feelings with me. As I sat with this and felt into it, I realised there was a lot I wanted to learn about myself. I felt like I was about to step into the next layer of self-discovery.

I'd been feeling quite numb, still struggling to find joy in things at times and just going through the motions. I'm sure Rob thought I was just cranky, but I wasn't. I didn't feel much at all. I booked an appointment with my grief counsellor and felt a huge shift within myself. It was so powerful to take the time out to really connect with what was happening for me internally. Those sessions felt intense at times, with lots of tears shed, but I always felt better walking out than I did when I walked in. Participating in sand play therapy, the often nonverbal, hands-on therapeutic intervention that reflects a person's inner thoughts, feelings, emotions, struggles, and concerns is a powerful form of psychological work that facilitates the psyche's natural ability to heal. It was amazing to feel and experience the depths this work could reach and what it could uncover.

I felt a deeper connection within myself after a few sessions, and within a month I was feeling so much better. Being able to recognise when I needed additional support was essential to my healing and growth.

Almost three years since Ella left, I felt there was no end to the journey through grief. I mean, it changes as time moves on, but it never goes away.

Rob and I were due to head to Nepal a few months later for three weeks of trekking the Annapurna Circuit. I knew it would be life-changing and felt it was happening at the perfect time for us both, giving us space and time to be with ourselves in nature, experiencing the incredible diversity Nepal had to offer.

We were also about to move house—a massive transition for all of us. Leaving our home that we'd spent the majority of our lives with Ella in was hard. The energy in the house had been so different since she'd been gone, which of course was to be expected. It felt very stuck and stagnant to me. Rob and I hardly ever watched television. It just felt too hard to sit on the lounge without Ella every night like we used to, watching her favourite shows, like Master Chef and Australia's Got Talent. It was just not the same. How could it be? We didn't have a lot of spare time, so most nights, if we weren't too tired, we would read or listen to music. The boys spent most of their time in their bedrooms when they weren't at work, and we only came together to eat our dinner when they were home. It was a struggle for me there.

I didn't know how I was going to pack up Ella's room and all her things that were still just the way she'd left them. I walked into her room and looked at the Lego˚ she'd put together with her own hands. *I want it to stay intact forever.* Her favourite pillow pets sat on her bed. I clung desperately to every little piece of her that remained in my reach.

I decided I would give her beanie bear collection to her friends and had each of them choose one they would like to keep in memory of her. I knew how special this was for them. I had lots of her toys and didn't want to keep them all to myself. Sharing them with the people she loved felt good.

The time had come. I needed to start packing up her room. It was so very hard, but it was another step forward. I took my time over many weeks, through lots of tears, and packed into boxes everything I wanted to keep. I had clients going on a trip to Bali soon who were taking donations to orphanages. Deciding Ella would love to help other children in any way she could, I packed up some of her clothes and shoes that I was prepared to let go of, while holding on to a few precious pieces that I will keep forever (like her onesie cow print pjs).

I was so blessed to have a beautiful patchwork quilt made from Ella's clothes by a lovely friend. Each piece reminds me of times we were together when she wore those clothes, bringing beautiful memories flooding back. Sometimes when I look at it, I can hear her laughter and see her radiant smile. I wasn't ready to hand over any of her clothes when my friend first offered to make the quilt. It took about twelve months before I could, and I'm so glad I did, because I now have the most precious piece of creative artwork, put together with so much love. I treasure it with all my heart.

The idea to move house felt right for us all. Originally, we were going to build a house and had put a deposit on a block of land. When we went to sign the contracts for the land something wasn't right with the paperwork, so we left it to get fixed up and said we'd be back the following week. Meanwhile, one particular house kept popping up in my searches and on social media. I was so drawn to the house that I showed Rob, Sam and Tim. They thought I was crazy. We'd spent a lot of time planning the house we wanted to build, with a large pinboard displaying our ideas and magazines of sustainable living options sprawled over our coffee table. Yet I couldn't help but feel we had to go and look at that house. Something pulled me toward it so strongly. Rob was keen too. The boys didn't know what to think. But if there was one thing I'd learnt over the past few years, it was to listen to my gut instinct, and right then it was very strong.

The next day we organised an inspection. We both fell in love with it. By the end of that week we'd made an offer on the house and it had been accepted. It was a bit more than we'd originally planned on spending, but we knew in our hearts that Ella had guided us to the house. It was perfect. Our one-acre piece of paradise. Upstairs had two bedrooms, with a small loft room that we could use as Ella's special space, so I had somewhere to be where I felt she was present and part of our new home. I felt like that little room would be my meditation space. The boys could have a bedroom each upstairs, with their own bathroom, and we had a bedroom and study downstairs.

With a magnificent timber verandah all the way around the house and a view of the mountains, it was a beautiful transition and made it a lot easier for me to cope with moving. The energy was so serene and peaceful, and it even had a granny flat that could be used for my clinic, totally separate from the house, and it was only a five-minute drive to Rob's workshop. It was perfect.

There was an amazing huge deciduous tree at the front of the house. It had no leaves at all when we first saw it, but I knew when it was in full bloom it would be truly stunning. I called it my tree of life.

Packing up our old house brought up so many emotions to process each day. I knew in my heart we were doing the right thing for all of us, it was just happening very quickly. Our house took a few weeks to sell, so we decided to move into our new home as soon as it settled. It was amazing! As I stood on the verandah looking out to the mountains, I felt Ella's presence so deeply. There was such a deep feeling of calmness there. This was part of our medicine.

As with most moves, it was a little hectic, but it was good to have extra time to go back to the old house as much as I needed, and to finally see it empty. After each visit I became a little more detached from the house and realised Ella was no longer there, she was with us. She would always be with us, wherever we went. By the time our house was sold, I was comfortable and content to let it go. We took all our memories with us in our hearts.

The shift in energy was positive for everyone. I felt us all coming back together a little more as a family unit in our new home. Tim's girlfriend Maddie moved in with us also. It was lovely for me to have some female energy around. Maddie came into Tim's life the year after we lost Ella. I believe Ella sent her to him, for them both to heal in different ways. She is a beautiful addition to our family and I have so much love for her. She is funny, cheeky, very honest and has a playful, childlike innocence that draws you to her.

After being in our new home for only six weeks, Rob and I left for our trip to Nepal. It was an amazing three weeks of cultural exploration, hiking, physical challenges and connection to some of the most beautiful people we had ever met. The Nepalese are friendly, warm and welcoming. As we looked around at the conditions some of them lived in, we realised just how lucky we were and felt an even stronger appreciation of life.

During this time we took a flight over Mount Everest. It was the most amazing feeling to be flying in the clouds at the same level of the incredible mountains that people actually climb! Looking out the window, overwhelmed by the beauty surrounding me, my eyes filled with tears. It felt like heaven. I sensed I was closer than ever to Ella in that moment. The clouds were like fairy floss as we soared above them. It was so peaceful. I closed my eyes and took a picture memory that imprinted on my soul so I would never forget.

Three weeks was a good length of time for us both to be able to relax and switch off from the pressures of work and moving house, and a great reset before returning to our new home.

So much was shifting around us through the choices we were making.

≈

Reflection Song: Ocean—Michael Benjamin

26

Taking the Plunge

'The way to become one with the Universe is to trust it.'
Alan Watts

April 2018

Today is the beginning of another chapter in my life. Today I start my training to become a KaHuna Massage Therapist.

The training was held at High Spirits retreat in Kin Kin, Queensland, the same place where I'd attended the women's retreat. Being there brought up a lot of memories for me. This was not a bad thing, but a reminder of the place I was in almost three years ago, not just physically but emotionally.

I was still not feeling the joy and happiness I wanted to feel in my life, and I wasn't sure how to bring it back. Part of me kept thinking it left when I lost Ella, and I know some of it did, but I was starting to feel that I had disconnected to some of it long before that.

Maybe this went deeper? This was what I needed to discover.

There are many processes that encourage connection with self and others. Allowing people to fully connect with me is a very emotional process and often painful. Allowing people in to see the depth of my pain hurt, yet I knew

I needed to do so to continue the healing process. I was exactly where I needed to be.

Being back there felt like my second home. Being surrounded by people who loved and accepted me for who I was without any judgement or expectations was a truly beautiful environment to be in.

Letting go of attachment to others is challenging and losing the people I love has a huge connection to fear for me. I know I cannot fully love from a place of fear, and that was one of the reasons I was there—to learn how to love from a place of pure love without clinging on through fear.

Sending unconditional love to the people I love and allowing them to find their own way, learn their own life lessons and find their own blessings in life is the most beautiful gift I can give them. Letting my children and husband know that I trust them to be able to make good choices for themselves, while always being here to support and guide them if that is what they need, is all I can do to be the parent and wife I want to be.

This is how I want to show up in the world.

I never want my children to feel they have to adhere to family conditioning that has been passed down through generations. I want them to be able to find out who they are as young men in this world through each choice they make, to do something with their lives that brings them joy, whatever that may be. The anguish they have endured has changed and shaped their lives forever. All I wish for them is that they find happiness and listen to their own hearts each step of their journey.

Going into retreat space helped me to see clearly, but never could I have imagined just how clearly.

One night, as the moon rose into the sky, we set up the hall to work in groups of three. We were performing an energetic massage, where you don't physically touch the body, but move energy around the body in its energy field. Wrapped tightly in a blanket, like in a cocoon, I felt like a baby, warm, snug and secure as I lay on the massage table. A meditation played which helped to shift any fear we were holding in our bodies. I sometimes had difficultly dropping into meditation, as my mind liked to go pretty wild at times, but I did, and I started to feel a lot of emotion arising in my body as energy began to move around.

Following my breath, I sensed a deep connection taking place. My body started to twitch, and my limbs started to shake. Soon, my whole body was shaking uncontrollably on the table. All I could feel was the trapped fear in my body rising, looking for a way out. I was not scared about the process taking place. I felt it was coming from a depth within me that I hadn't felt before. As I allowed people to support me and gave myself permission to let go and receive fully, my emotions became stronger and stronger. Fear. Fear of losing the people I love. Fear that if I was to follow my path, maybe there would be other people I would lose. Fear that my emotions were too much for others.

I fully trusted what was happening and allowed it to move through my body. I'm unsure how long this process went on for, but as the meditation came to an end for most people in the room, my process continued, and my body went on shaking. I imagine it felt similar to some sort of convulsion. It felt like I had no control over it. Even as I became slightly aware of what was happening around me, my body still moved, full of emotion and shifting energy. It was intense.

As the energy started to settle, my body slowed itself down. Eventually I was able to sit up slowly on the edge of the table and breathe deeply. Helped to get off the table,

I discovered my legs felt like they no longer worked. I could hardly walk. Still, no fear was present. The trust I felt was unwavering and I knew in my heart that everything was unfolding exactly as it was meant to.

I was helped outside to sit in the fresh air of the night. Not fully present in my body, I was somewhere else, disconnected from myself. I was in a space I knew well. Almost numb. I'd been there before.

Then I heard the beautiful, soft voice of Mette, the founder and lead facilitator of High Spirits, 'Kim, you've been here before, and you have a choice of how long you want to stay here in this space.'

I was left to sit with another facilitator who was there to support and comfort me as I slowly came back into my body. This time, I made a conscious choice that I was not going to stay trapped in the darkness and numbness that fear had previously left me feeling. It was time to change that pattern. I started to gradually feel my body again, my feet, legs, fingers and toes. Breathing slowly and deeply, I started to talk. I just allowed whatever was present to come out and spoke freely. I talked about moments, emotions and feelings that had been held deep within me for a long, long time and things started to shift. I felt different. Very different.

Exhausted, but different.

The closest I've ever come to having any sort of bodily experience like that was when I attended a seven-day Shamanic Retreat the previous year and journeyed into another world where I connected with Ella. I didn't want to come back into my body after that journey; I wanted to stay with her. That time, as my body twitched and shook, I resisted the pull to return. I was afraid I would never have the opportunity to see her again. Fear.

This felt slightly familiar.

As I sat outside in the cool night air, my energy felt like it was starting to rebalance within my body. I could feel each cell gently settling, recalibrating, finding homeostasis. I was encouraged to re-join the group and do some gentle movement to help move any residual energy that needed shifting.

I felt very strange and was so tired.

After sleeping all night, I woke early the next morning. I still didn't feel I was totally in my body. Making my way outside before the sun rose, I was surrounded by darkness while the damp dew of the early morning caressed my feet. I felt as though my physical body was moving, but my spirit body was walking in front of me. That is the only way I can explain it. It was a little weird.

I looked up to see the stars still in the sky. It was like seeing stars for the very first time. It was amazing. So beautiful. Looking at the flowers along the path, I saw them in full three-dimensional detail that I hadn't experienced before. One of the most incredible, awe-inspiring moments of my life, it was like I was seeing everything for the very first time.

All my senses felt heightened and alive. I felt like I'd been reborn!

It took around four hours that morning until I fully felt that my body and spirit had realigned.

I had been transformed in some way and it felt so different to what I was used to.

What an amazing experience and awareness for me to have—to know that so much energy can be shifted from the body. Even though I felt like I had no control over my body during the experience, in the end I had to consciously choose to come back into my body.

I never at any stage felt scared or panicked, as I trusted the process entirely and knew I was surrounded by people who could support me and send me nothing but love.

Allowing myself to be vulnerable in that space, while not easy, felt safe. Safe. That was the feeling I'd been searching for—I just wanted to feel safe.

In the past, it had been a fine balance to feel into how long to allow myself to sit in emotions when they arose, ensuring I gave myself enough time to process what I was feeling so it completed its cycle and wasn't pushed back down into my body, while not getting stuck in any heavy energy for too long.

Sometimes, shifting the energy for me at home can be as simple as moving to another part of the house or yard, going for a walk, having a cup of tea, meditating, listening to some music, dancing, singing or chanting, or focussing on my other senses—like smelling the flowers, getting out some essential oils, or having something to eat that is nurturing and grounding for my body, or even at times allowing myself to lie down and rest.

I try to never go into anything with expectations. There was certainly no way I could have anticipated what was to change for me during my first levels of KaHuna training! I have so much gratitude for those who were with me that night, and to myself for trusting the process and allowing it to fully unfold.

This was a path I would continue. With seven levels of training, KaHuna was now part of who I was becoming. I wanted to share this with as many people as I could in the world—even my small part of the world. Connection and healing through touch is so powerful. I just wish everyone realised the innate healing potential their own bodies have and the incredible healing power touch has. When I am massaging and in the right space physically, mentally, spiritually, and energetically, everything aligns within me and I am sending love and healing into the world with my hands and my heart. Sending this energy out into the world, connecting with one person at a time, will change the world, little by little. This I know is true.

As human beings, a social species, we are wired for connection. Love and a sense of belonging are some of the most important needs we must fulfil, but when we carry a lot of emotional wounds, it makes it difficult for walls to come down and hearts to open fully to feel deep connection. We walk around 'thinking' we are protecting ourselves, when what we're really doing is preventing the love we long for to even be able to enter our lives.

When we start to have this self-awareness, we have a beautiful opportunity to begin to look deeply within ourselves and recognise patterns of behaviour that are no longer supporting the life we are attempting to create. It is only then that we can make a conscious choice to step into this space and take full responsibility for changing these patterns ourselves.

Loving with an open heart, where love flows freely, is only possible when fear is not present. When fear is present so is attachment. Don't ever confuse attachment with love.

Love without attachment is the purest form of love.

Reflection Song: Just Fine (Alternate Version)—Desirée Dawson

27

Leave Your Negativity and Your Shoes at the Door

*'The answer to every adversity lies in
courageously moving forward with faith.'*
Edmond Mbiaka

I missed Rob, my boys and Maddie terribly. Being away from them was challenging, but I knew it was also part of my growth and I trusted in the process of what I'd chosen to do. It just felt so right in so many ways.

Coming home from any retreat environment is challenging. I'd been away from the outside world and all the external distractions for a whole week. Something in me had changed, and I now had to navigate back into an environment that felt the same as when I'd left. Adapting, while remembering to hold onto the life changing commitments I'd made to myself, was essential for my growth. I had changed on a cellular level and let go of things that I recognised did not serve any purpose in my present life, and it was impossible to go backwards. There are things I never want to let go of and people I never want to leave behind, but letting go opens space for new things to arrive and is all part of moving forward with faith.

Having a deeper connection to myself and my needs as a person, I tried to honour them as much as I could, while being aware of communicating this to those I loved who I'd come home to.

Honest and clear communication around how you are feeling goes a long way in relationships and helps those you love to be able to understand and support you. They hadn't experienced what I had, and at times, I know it must have been hard for them to understand where I was at and what had changed. I needed more quiet space and time alone. My ability to listen to negative comments and conversations was extremely limited (more than normal, that is) and I was very conscious of keeping my mind clear, my heart open and my energy calm and peaceful.

It was hard to describe some of the experiences to others who weren't there to feel the emotions and energy of the moment. Sometimes I just had to decide how much I really wanted to share, and with who. Even though it felt so exciting to have experienced the incredible moments that had changed my life in so many ways, they were very personal to me and sacred. The last thing I wanted to do was feel that by sharing and having someone not understand (how could they, these were my experiences, not theirs), or play down the importance of them for me, it could be detrimental to the processes I was still moving through as I tried to integrate back into this 'new normal'.

Or was it an 'old normal' that I'd lost connection to and sight of long ago? There was a deep, familiar feeling within. I found that this work, as I turned further inwards to look at myself and witnessed others do the same, was unique and personal to each individual person. Some of it just could not be shared with anyone.

It was time to decide what was best for my own growth and transformation.

I acknowledged that other people's opinions were just that. I knew never to allow them to be louder than my own inner voice.

Self-care is not just about making healthy, practical lifestyle choices. It also includes self-compassion, healthy boundaries, being connected and attuned to my needs and staying true to my values.

I'd started doing work to establish what my core values were a few years earlier. It truly changed my life, helping me to make decisions I'd struggled with in the past and to take action and move towards the life I wanted to live. It brought a stronger sense of stability and confidence to my life. I didn't have to second guess things anymore as they became so much clearer. When I'm having any sort of internal conflict, I simply go back to my values and re-align with them. This puts me in a space where I can be true to myself with every decision I make. It helps me to get to know myself and what my core beliefs are. My values guide me to live authentically, and when misaligned, imbalance is created within and around me and life can start to feel turbulent.

During this time, I started to understand why I'd felt so much anxiety in the past and its importance. The anxiety had been the unsettling feeling within me, screaming out for me to acknowledge that what was happening within or around me was not in alignment with my truth. That gut feeling, which would always try to send me messages through my cells that whatever was happening in the moment was not right for me. The unbalanced, strong vibration of anxiety, a force that would send my nervous system into overdrive with nauseating internal turmoil, racing heart and what felt like uncontrollable overthinking.

When I started to recognise this and had enough self-awareness to tune in with my values and connect with the sensations in my body, it gave me more confidence and trust to connect to my own intuition. I was able to start to calm myself internally and respond to situations, instead of reacting to them as soon as my nervous system was triggered into being defensive. This meant that sometimes I would have to remove myself from certain situations in order to change the patterns that my mind and body had become accustomed to being the normal way of life.

I spent more time quietening my own mind through meditation and being in nature. The result—I started to connect more deeply with my own wisdom, that sense of knowing that I was born with and did not have to question. It is a feeling that sits deep within my soul, in the centre of my body, at my core, keeping me balanced, aligned and at peace. It is a beautiful place to be.

Reflection Song: I Am—Satsang

28

I Am Back

'When I let go of what I am,
I become what I might be.
When I let go of what I have,
I receive what I need.'

Lao Tzu

April 2019

Twelve months after my first KaHuna training and I was back for more. In that time, I had introduced KaHuna/Lomi Lomi massage into my clinic alongside Holistic Kinesiology/Mind Body Connection sessions. I found that people who incorporated the massage into some of their sessions, or alternated their sessions between the two modalities, were starting to connect with themselves on a deeper level.

The healing power of touch through KaHuna was a major contributor to this outcome, along with the trust that it helped to develop between client and practitioner. Feeling vulnerable and staying open can only happen when a safe, nurturing environment has been created, opening the way for deeper healing and connection to self on so many levels. I feel honoured to be able to provide such a sacred space for people to step into.

This level of training was where we started to do underbody work, which always feels incredible to receive. Underbody massage consists of massaging the part of the body that is lying directly on the table. If you are lying on your stomach, the massage therapist is gliding their hand and arm through, between your stomach and the table. Coconut oil is used to assist in this process. This can often be an area that people have not had massaged before and it can be quite sensitive, having stored a lot of emotions for long periods of time.

If you've heard the saying that the 'gut is the second brain', this might help you to understand why this area of the body can be a little vulnerable. There are strong connections in the nervous system between the brain and the gastrointestinal system. Imbalances in your gut can send messages and signals to the brain that trigger mood changes and even contribute to the development of anxiety and depression.

Just have a think about what feelings and emotions could be stored in your own gut.

It was exciting to be learning more skills to take back to my clinic to share, and beautiful to be back in the High Spirits environment, meeting new people, connecting to like-minded souls, letting down our guards and going deeper within ourselves.

I had a realisation that was based around connection. I was struggling with allowing people to connect with me on a deeper level. You know when someone hugs you for just that little bit longer—long enough to start to stir emotions within you, long enough for you to actually feel, really feel. While I love deep connection, sometimes it felt overwhelming for me.

I didn't want to feel my own pain all the time. It was exhausting. There were many times I sat in that space with my pain, alone, but being with others in that space I often felt like I was a burden, too much. This awareness was powerful because it felt like I was not able to always be the truest version of myself in all situations and holding back was impacting all areas of my life.

So, of course, just so the Universe could test this theory out, it sent someone directly to me who gave me a beautiful long hug. I started to pull away after a short period of time as feelings and emotions began to rise, not wanting to become a blubbering mess in that moment. It was hard to allow myself to be held by a stranger. It was something I was not used to.

I love to do this for other people, holding others with love and compassion so they feel connected and know I am there for them. Holding this space for others feels natural, yet I was pulling away so I could not receive that from someone else. This awareness made me question the affect it was having on my relationships. I asked myself the question—*what is it that I don't want them to see or feel?*

It's the pain that lives deep inside my heart. Every time it is cracked open it hurts bad, yet I don't know that this will ever go away. So maybe this was just a way of me managing just how many times I had to cope with feeling this depth of pain?

I certainly didn't want to push emotions that needed to be felt down into my body, nor did I want to create illness and imbalance within myself. I wanted to be able to connect to people wholeheartedly, so how would I know what was a healthy balance for me?

Maybe that was the question that would be answered over the coming week?

Self-awareness helps me with self-reflection and enables me to see myself a little more clearly. Monitoring my inner world gives me the chance to sit with what is happening and dig a little deeper into what this might mean and why I have developed certain types of behaviour throughout my life. Stepping into this space of conscious awareness helps me to understand myself and look at options to change my long-term learnt patterns if they are not working well for me.

Part of the training was also detoxing the body by eating only whole, unprocessed foods with no nasties, moving, swimming, early morning saunas, walks and lots and lots of massage.

It is so important that my body can be a clean, clear vessel for energy to pass through when I am massaging. A few weeks before this training I started to cleanse my body, removing anything that didn't fit into the detox category, like tea, coffee, alcohol, processed foods, breads, and red meat. I also increased my water intake and drank lots of fresh lemon squeezed into hot water every morning. I already ate pretty healthily, but that preparation made it a little easier when arriving, as my body had already started the detox process. Sometimes that can make me feel pretty crap for the first few days as my body tries to adjust, with symptoms like headaches, constipation, upset stomach, body aches and pains, but when it all starts to shift and the inflammation in my body starts to reduce, I feel lighter and have so much more energy. My aches and pains disappear, and I wonder why the hell I didn't do this sooner.

That week we were also learning pregnancy massage, which I felt so blessed to be part of. A number of expecting ladies volunteered. It was such an honour to be able to connect with those beautiful women, each carrying another human being inside of them. Such a miracle, that a woman's body is capable of the incredible process that begins with conception to create new life.

I find it extraordinary that all the eggs a woman will ever carry form in her ovaries while she is a four-month-old foetus in the womb of her mother. This means that our cellular life begins as an egg in the womb of our grandmothers. Each of us spent up to five months in our grandmother's womb, as she in turn formed in the womb of her grandmother. This generational thread runs so far back through the lineage of women that have come before us.

I watched the demonstration with such love, realising how different my life was when I was carrying my own children. Soon enough, an intense feeling from deep within surfaced. Emotions were felt and suddenly I felt so much sadness, like my heart was breaking open. I took some deep breaths and managed to keep it 'under control'!

Who was I kidding?

We all placed our hands on a beautiful woman and the baby growing inside her belly, while one of the facilitators read a blessing. Tears rolled from my eyes. I had no control over the feeling—such a deep pain, sadness and grief rose from within for the loss of my little girl, the longing to have more children (which was no longer possible for me) and the realisation that I had given my power away so many years ago to doctors who removed my womb when I was only thirty-seven years old. I had handed over my trust to them, thinking at the time that I had no other options. If only I knew then what I know now.

I tried to recentre myself and breathe deeply, but it wasn't helping. I should have known better than to try and stuff pain back down into my body.

My body had a new way of processing my emotions, as things had been shifting over the past couple of years. Pushing them back down and supressing was no longer a pathway my body recognised or aligned with. A beautiful soul sister comforted me as I let go and allowed myself to be held. My tears continued to fall as I surrendered into her loving arms (one of the lessons I was sent there to embrace).

We moved into small groups to massage each other. I was first on the table to receive. My body and soul continued to shed, my emotions slowly releasing until a gentle calmness washed through me as I witnessed the unique wisdom of my own body and the power of gentle, loving touch once again. It knew when it had to let go and it knew when it was time to realign itself. I just had to give it the space to do so.

It was then that I was able to re-enter a space where I could give again.

Just like that, in the space of an hour I felt like my cup was empty, I gave myself the opportunity and space to feel, release, receive and refill my cup, and was blessed to be able to join in on a group massage on one of the expecting women. A powerful reminder of how everything is always shifting and changing. I massaged her beautiful belly that held her unborn child with so much love. It truly was a special experience. The love and compassion I felt was indescribable. I felt that the joy inside me that I had lost connection with had been reignited.

The woman I massaged had experienced an interrupted pregnancy through miscarriage before carrying the baby present in her belly that day. I felt her loss when I first connected with her. During the massage experience and the love that she felt, she shared with us all at the end that she had seen her angel baby leave her body and float above her, before leaving to move into the next world. She described it as the most beautiful, peaceful experience she'd ever felt, knowing her womb was no longer grieving the loss of her precious baby. This meant that her child now living inside of her could arrive in the world from a place of pure love, without being attached to the grief that had been surrounding it from the precious life previously lost in the womb of its mother.

That moment was incredibly transforming for me as my pain moved into love and joy, all through the power of connection and touch. I felt Ella with me and felt a gentle gracefulness enter my body. I realised joy could be felt in so many different ways. It did not always show up as being boisterous and loud, through laughter and dance, but could also be quiet and peaceful, beautiful and calm. That is what joy felt like for me in that moment.

When you let go of the expectation of how you think things 'should' look or feel, you get to experience the reality and realness of the spectrum of emotions in whatever way they present themselves in your life.

After my experience the previous year, on my first level of KaHuna training, I learnt that allowing my emotions to release when I felt them rise, not stuffing them down for later, was the key to shifting my energy and returning to a place where I could hold myself with unconditional love.

When we have pain that stands in the way of connection with others and ourselves, we can never get to the place where we are able to fully receive or give. There are just too many roadblocks to get through. Allowing ourselves to feel and process these feelings in a safe place where we are supported and loved is key to being able to grow and move forward with an open heart.

This experience once again instilled my beliefs and strengthened my trust in my own body and its ability to heal. It helped me to let go a little more to experience even deeper connections in my life, inviting joy back in and strengthening my purpose to provide more spaces for people to have the opportunity to do the same.

Reflection Song: Break On Me—Keith Urban

29

Shake It Up

'Forgiveness is the gift you give yourself.'
Tony Robbins

As we continued through our days, learning, processing, healing, moving and connecting, my body started to feel different. I was so sore when I arrived. Everything ached and I felt stiff and inflexible, like nothing was flowing. By day four I could still feel a lot of physical pain, but it was changing. I thought the previous day's process may have helped with that a little more. I should have known there was more to come.

While learning the massage techniques of KaHuna, we were also giving our bodies the opportunity to heal. Being a KaHuna Massage Therapist for me is not just about giving a massage, it's about being able to connect with someone on a deeper level through the body and be in a space where everything flows naturally. There is no thought process. It feels like magic. When the person you're massaging feels safe, comfortable and at ease, they can relax as they focus on nothing but their breath and allow the therapist to move their body freely. The experience can be incredibly profound—to allow yourself to fully trust and release.

For me, it takes a little while to slow down the thoughts in my mind when I am receiving, especially if I'm in a learning environment. However, the more massages I receive, the easier it becomes. I'd never experienced a massage like KaHuna before. My first one was in 2015, the year after Ella left, by a very powerful, gentle man. I had a number of incredible massages with him that enabled me to let go of so much pain and grief that was stored in my body.

A year later, when I was talking with him, he told me that during the first massage I had received from him, Ella had tried to get a message to me through him. He said it happened so quickly and strongly, but he was not ready or prepared for it and blocked it. I know in hindsight that I was probably not ready for it either at that time, yet I always remember it and wonder what she wanted to say to me.

I knew it was hard for her to reach me through my pain and that she looked for other avenues to get messages to me, usually through other people she could channel through.

It is such a gift to be able to share this experience with others.

Moving the body, not just through massage, is a fantastic way to shift energy and emotions. Think about how you feel when you're dancing, walking, running or playing with little children outside in the fresh air with no limitations. The body likes to move. It is fluid. Have you noticed how your body feels when you haven't moved or exercised for a period of time? Things start to become stiff, stuck and energy starts to become stagnant. When the body feels rigid, energy is not flowing freely, and this can affect our physical and emotional bodies. In Chinese medicine stagnant energy (Qi) is one of the most basic causes that disease develops from. There has to be a smooth flow of energy in order to be happy and healthy.

We were doing a meditation process through movement, based around the teachings of OSHO, the Indian guru who emphasised the importance of free thought, meditation, mindfulness, love, celebration, courage, creativity and humour. Rajneesh (OSHO) presented meditation not just as a practice, but as a state of awareness to be maintained in every moment, a total awareness that awakens the individual from the sleep of mechanical responses conditioned by beliefs and expectations.

I was very interested and curious about this process and went in with an open heart and mind. We were blindfolded through this experience and stood on our own mats, so we had a concept of how much space we each had.

The music started. First, we shook our whole bodies to music and made as much vocal sound as we felt we needed to for about fifteen minutes. It felt like a long time! I started to feel the energy moving around my body. It felt good once I moved past the state of being self-conscious in any way. As I let go of any ego around what other people might be thinking or doing, I brought my full awareness back and immersed myself fully in the practice. It would have been impossible to experience the fullness of this process from any other space than deep connection with myself.

Second, we danced for fifteen minutes to music—still blindfolded. This felt like it took a little longer for energy to start to move around my body, then I began to open into an expansion of freedom that I had not experienced before. My body moved naturally with ease and openness.

Then we stopped and stood still for fifteen minutes while listening to a meditation.

I struggled to stand and connect deeply with the meditation and felt a little distracted. Then I got hot. Really hot. *How can I be feeling this hot?* I hoped someone might open a door so I could feel just a little bit of fresh air, but no one did.

Then I felt really hungry.

I started to think about food and what I'd like to eat.

Then I felt sick, like I was going to throw up.

Then I felt like I was going to pass out.

My body felt like it was in some sort of sensory overload and I was feeling everything in a very short moment in time.

My breath became fast and shallow as I lowered myself to the floor.

My whole body started to shake.

I was aware that everyone else was still standing. I still had my blindfold on.

The movement my body displayed was something I had no control over.

My body had taken over my mind.

Was I having some sort of convulsion? My eyes rolled back in my head.

I was no longer there, not in that room anymore.

One of the facilitators was talking to me. She had removed my blindfold and was asking me to look at her.

I could hear her calmly saying my name, but felt like I was looking straight through her as my eyes rolled back in my head again. Eventually, I was able to bring my eyes into alignment with hers, to make a connection with another human being.

I looked into her eyes and my body slowly stopped shaking and started to settle to sporadic twitching.

All I could do was focus on her eyes.

I lay on the mat until my body settled. Until there was no movement.

I was still. My body was recalibrating.

After a while I was slowly led outside, my legs like jelly. I knelt on the grass, my hands clutching at the earth like an animal, desperately trying to ground myself in some way. I stayed in that position for what felt like a very long time, until I slowly brought my body into an upright seated position.

I felt very weird, different.

Exhausted, I just wanted to go to sleep, so I stayed outside for a while, breathing in the cool air.

Led back into the room, I wrapped myself in a blanket and lay down, trying to breathe deeply, but as soon as my body started to relax again, I felt my eyes roll back in my head again and my right leg began to shake.

I needed to sit up.

I was helped to sit up against a wall and given a warm cup of herbal tea with honey.

I concentrated on the feeling of the warmth as it engulfed my hands, holding the warm mug close to my chest and feeling the heat against my heart.

It was comforting.

It felt like I was sitting in space.

I listened to the meditation playing in the background as the rest of the group lay on their mats, blindfolded, unaware of what had just taken place.

The meditation playing was Ho'oponopono—Ochre Cord Cutting.

Ho'oponopono is a Hawaiian tradition used to release our energy streams with others.

We do this through the mantra:

> I'm Sorry
> Please forgive me
> Thank You
> I Love You.

As I sat in that space and listened, two people came into my awareness.

Craig, my ex-husband, and my husband, Rob.

I received the clearest message that I needed to write a letter to Craig. This was something that had come up before for me. Now it needed to be done. I wasn't sure if it was something I actually needed to give to him, but I knew I needed to write it, to set myself free.

As I asked what I needed to say, the message was clear:

> I'm Sorry
> Please forgive me
> Thank You
> I Love You.
>
> I am sorry our marriage was not the way we both envisioned and hoped it to be.
> Please forgive me for anything I ever did that caused you pain.
> Thank you. I am grateful for everything we experienced together and the three incredible children we created.
> I will always have love for you—you are the father of my children.

I needed to do the same thing for Rob, but in person.

Forgiveness is a gift you give yourself, and the gift I had just received was the wisdom to know what it was that I needed to do to set myself free. Forgiving is not about condoning any hurtful actions or behaviour of others; it is about releasing the power that you have allowed this to have over you and your life.

As this took place a warm, gentle sensation moved through my body.

I continued to process what my body had physically gone through. I do know on a soul level that my ability to fully trust the process of my own body is probably the reason why my body had such an intense response. I am willing to let go of whatever it is my body is holding onto if it shows me a sign that this is what I need to do to move forward.

I felt like a snow globe that had been shaken up on the inside and was slowly resettling back into a new, realigned version of myself. It was a new feeling, but also one I recognised from long ago.

Everything had slowed down. Internally and externally.

I knew in my heart and soul that the process I'd just experienced had released trauma from my body that had never before had the opportunity to be felt and processed fully. During and after this, I felt a very strong sense of ancestral healing taking place. There had been a deep ache inside me that made me so sad, knowing I'd brought children into the world who'd had trauma passed down through their DNA from past generations. As far as I knew, no one before me in my family had delved into the depth of healing this trauma to change the cycles and patterns from the past. As each generation emerged, it had its own challenges and trauma to process and store in the body to add to this.

Maybe this was also part of my purpose?

Another reminder to keep turning the wheels in motion to heal some of the generational trauma within our family. My children were now in their twenties, and I didn't want this ancestral pain and conditioning to be passed down to another generation, a generation I had created. I knew the only thing I could do was to decide what I was prepared to do to heal myself, and hope that had a ripple effect out towards those I loved so dearly, that they may see and feel the impact of this energetically. All I had the power to do was to decide what I needed to do for myself, my own healing, my own life, and the decisions I made each day to live in a way that felt purposeful and peaceful.

I knew it was all happening at exactly the right time. I was not ready for any of this before—before Ella left.

My oldest son, Sam, is very open to trying different modalities and therapies to help him process his feelings and emotions in ways he feels are right for him. Tim comes across as being very closed to this at times, or should I say, he makes out he is! However, I know that energetically my work impacted his life, just by being around and witnessing the changes that were unfolding through me. We often had oracle cards sitting around the house, and it was very interesting when he'd randomly pull a card from a deck, then proceed to tell me it was all a load of crap as he received a spot-on message like a big slap in the face. We'd both just smile at each other with a deep connection and knowing, as he'd tell me it was all bullshit and laugh.

They both have their own journeys and I acknowledge that. I honour them for being who they are as individual young men. They will do their own healing in their own time, if and when they are ready.

It is so important for me that I do not pass down behaviours that I have developed from my conditioning and old belief systems that have been carried through my ancestral lines for generations. This includes my own grief and pain, for that is not theirs to carry.

I believe generational healing is essential to a person's health and wellbeing. Every person holds within their DNA physical and energetic remnants that have been passed down through their genetic lineage. It is understood that trauma experienced by earlier generations can influence the structure of our genes.

Even though I know some of this has already been passed down to my children, I also know the best I can do is to lead by example and show them there are many ways to acknowledge and heal this trauma. Releasing these inherited patterns will help me to free myself to be able to express, experience and engage more fully in who I am. My wish for my children is that they grow up being their own unique selves and find a place in the world where they feel part of something that brings them contentment and happiness, living their lives like there is no tomorrow.

To me, that is the purpose of being alive.

When I arrived home I called Craig and asked him to meet me at Ella's gravesite. We talked, and without any expectations, I gave him an envelope with the letter I'd written inside.

We said goodbye and drove away.

I felt a tremendous sense of lightness, love for myself and gratitude for him.

I don't know what he did with it, or if he even read it. It made no difference to me.

Reflection Song: Forgiveness—Trevor Hall, Luka Lesson

30

Integration

'If you want to cure the world, don't emanate fear - emanate love.'
                                    Ram Dass

A week after I returned from KaHuna training, we were away camping with friends. I'd had eight KaHuna massage clients booked in for the week I returned, a great way to share my new skills with others and keep the energy flowing, but in hindsight, maybe not the best thing for me as I tried to re-integrate. Because I hadn't given myself much space when I first returned, I was in transition while on holiday with other people, which was challenging.

When I left the retreat, I was told it could take anywhere from seven to twenty-one days (minimum) to transition and re-adjust. Some days my body felt weird, tingly, like there was a lot of energy moving, trying to settle and find equilibrium.

Returning from these trainings and experiences, I always found myself so much more open to everything, like my heart had expanded. On my first night home from retreat, Rob offered to give me a massage, which I thought was such a beautiful gesture for us to reconnect (we'd done a weekend Lomi Lomi massage course together a few years earlier). During that experience I felt half asleep and like I was in a dream state. Allowing myself to fully receive from my husband as he gave from his heart, I had one of the most beautiful encounters I've ever had. I saw so many different colours in the room—red, orange, yellow, green, blue, purple and then a beautiful, pure white light surrounded us both. It was incredible. I wanted it to last forever.

The experiences you can have when your heart is fully open, your mind is clear, your walls are down, you feel safe and are both flowing from a place of unconditional love for yourself and the other person are indescribable. There is a whole other world to explore when you step into this deep, connective state of being.

Some people ask why I put myself through some of the things I've experienced. That's easy for me to answer, but maybe not as easy to do at times.

I do what I do because it makes my life incredible, clears blockages that get in the way of experiencing life fully, provides space for connection and permission for my walls to come down. It allows my heart to open and give to others, while enabling me to receive on a deep level as I get to know my true self and tune in to how I want to step into each day that I am gifted to live here on earth.

It is not just healing me but healing those around me. It helps to heal my personal trauma and any generational trauma that has been passed on through me. It is liberating and freeing, powerful and beautiful. It is me acknowledging that I am worthy, and capable of much more than I have ever allowed myself to be in the past. There is a bigger picture to all of this than what I experience on a personal level. It is what I have been called to do and I do not question it. I just trust the journey as opportunities arise that I am guided to be part of.

It helps me to remember why I am here.

Rob has also received amazing healing through KaHuna massage. I believe that even if you never practice this type of massage on anyone else, the level of personal development and healing that can take place as this incredible gift is passed on cannot be replaced and will be an experience that will change you forever.

The holiday was a little different for us, and I noticed Rob hadn't talked about work as much as he usually did when we were away, which was a nice change, as it was usually the focus of most conversations. Owning his own company and being switched on 24/7 for so long made it a hard habit to get out of when you're only on holiday for one week. He often said he was waiting for the next 'Big Bang' each time the phone rang. This was not a great place to be living from. His nervous system was constantly on alert and the long-term impacts of that worried me a lot.

We'd had longer holidays in the past, up to three weeks at a time, and the only way he was able to truly relax and switch off was if he didn't have his phone with him, which meant he had to rely on someone else to take all the calls. He's the sort of person who likes to do things himself and know they are done properly. That's a treasured attribute and has been great for business because he is so reliable, but I wasn't sure how long he could keep that up. He was tired and constantly trying to keep people happy, even at the cost of his own health and happiness—not a good combination.

I struggled to be around negative energy, and after that KaHuna training I found it even more difficult. I made a conscious decision not to participate or step into the lower vibrational energy field negativity created. It's such a heavy energy to be around; it drags me down and doesn't sit comfortably within me or serve any positive purpose.

Everything has a vibration—every word that comes out of our mouths, every interaction we have with others, every emotion we feel and everything in nature. We all have a choice of what vibration we want to project into the world and the vibration we want to be part of each day.

Working in a clinic environment as I do, it's important that I can keep my vibration at a balanced level to be able to sustain my energy to get through my day without feeling depleted. That took me a while to figure out! My morning routine was essential to ensure my body was filled with fresh air and good nutrients, was fluid after some sort of movement, stable and grounded, and my mind was clear after taking time to connect to myself through meditation. This enabled me to sit with people in a safe space and support them daily, even when their own energy was heavy at times. I didn't take any of it on, because of how I had taken care of myself first.

You always need to put your own oxygen mask on first before you can help others.

Now I can feel just as energized when I finish my day in clinic as when I started.

That's balance.

It was all about making changes and choices that would serve me best. If that meant not being around negative people, then I had to ensure that was reduced within my life to assist me to manage this.

An optimist, I like to look on the bright side of life. I am hopeful and confident about my future and I believe anything is possible.

> **When I feel I have equilibrium and am in good balance I am happy, positive, driven and enthusiastic. I have a genuine love of life, even with a broken heart. I am learning it is possible to have both.**

When I'm passionate about something and it feels right for me, I put my heart and soul into channeling my energy into it so it can unfold as it's meant to. When I feel in alignment with an idea or vision I have, I trust the energy that lies behind it. I don't always know what it's going to look like, but I put it out there and work it out as I go along, knowing I don't have to have all the answers before I start. It's a great way to show how committed I am to myself.

Equally, when I'm out of balance, I usually find that fear and anxiety start to creep back in and feelings of not being good enough can arise. Then one of two things can happen:

1. I try to control my external environment, in order to feel safe. If I feel like I have that under control, then surely everything will be ok?
OR
2. I withdraw. I go quiet and feel I have nothing valuable to offer.

When I feel either of these things happening, I now have the awareness of *why* it is happening and I realise these are old patterns at play that no longer serve me. They are old stories that sometimes play on repeat in my mind, activated or triggered in some way.

Taking time out to sit with it and process what is really going on in my body and in my mind is the only way I can make long term changes for the future.

That is when I write.

I look at what thoughts are running through my mind and question if they are true. I check in with how those thoughts make me feel and how I would feel without them.

I breathe. I meditate. I find stillness in nature, and if I need to, I move my body by dancing, stretching, walking or doing yoga.

Usually, once I've taken some time out to do this, I can see so much more clearly. It is only in this space that I can get this clarity.

Reflection Song: Rise Up—Andra Day

31

Friendships

'A friend is someone who helps you when you are down. And if they can't, they lay down beside you and listen.'
A. A. Milne

Friendships are such interesting, diverse relationships in so many ways. I have friends I've known since school who I hardly ever see, yet I know they'd be there in a heartbeat if I needed them. I have friends I see regularly, maybe every few months, and lifetime friends who've been through hell and back with me and I know I could call on any time of the day or night.

And then there are those very few friends you meet out of the blue and just know you've been here together before. Those are where the real conversations come in. The deep and meaningful, raw stuff that connects souls together, the ones who make you feel, instead of think. These friendships are the best, and I am one of the lucky ones to have some of these.

When I lost Ella, I could not believe how many people reached out and contacted me. I know it was out of love and compassion, most of the time. People's hearts were breaking for me as a mother, and for my family, and they didn't know what to do.

I did, however, find it very interesting that I had people trying to befriend me on social media who I'd not previously been friends with.

Once, in the middle of a shopping centre, I even had someone apologise to me for something they felt bad about that had happened between us in the past that had never been resolved for them. Would she have ever approached me if Ella was still alive? I found it hard to understand and didn't spend too much time trying to analyse it, but it certainly made me wonder about some people's intentions at times.

> **I do believe people do the best they can with what they've got, and this also relates to emotional intelligence.**

I've had a lot of things said to me since losing Ella. One day, one of my good friends asked me, 'What are the three worst things you could say to someone who loses a child?'

I could only answer this from a place of personal experience.

The three worst things that were said to me were:

1. Lucky you have another two children!!! (*Because obviously that makes things so much better?*)
2. At least you know the reason why she died, that has to make it easier… ! (*Rule Number 1: NEVER compare grief!*)
3. You just have to be strong and keep going. (*Do I?*)

She also asked me what the three best things that people did, or could have done, to support me and my family were:

1. Talk about Ella—she will always be part of our lives. Share your memories with us and don't change the subject because it feels uncomfortable for you. This is our life. This is our daughter. That will NEVER change.
2. Show up. Be fully present, without any expectations. Be happy to sit in silence and be patient, listen and be accepting of strong emotions, even if it is uncomfortable for you, and don't ever be offended by anything a grieving person says. It is not about you.
3. Do the practical things. Cook meals or clean the house. These may not feel like you are doing much, but for a mother, it means a lot. To know my boys were being fed and looked after when I was not capable of doing that was a massive weight off my shoulders and felt like a little less guilt I had to carry at that time.

These are just a few of the best and worst experiences for me.

≈

Reflection Song: Count on Me—Joy Oladokun

32

Mother's Day

*'Being a mother is learning about strengths you
didn't know you had and dealing with fears
you didn't know existed.'*
                               Linda Wooten

May 2019

A friend asked me what Mother's Day was like for me. No one had ever asked me that before, but she wasn't afraid to ask the hard questions. Five years on and I'd never given it too much thought. I just tried to grin and bear it, feeling grateful for the two beautiful sons I had, while feeling broken for the daughter who was no longer here.

I was sitting on a train when I was asked that question, on my way to Sydney to do a weekend of training in Psychodrama. I hadn't even realised it was Mother's Day on that weekend when I initially booked into the training, but trusted I was there for a reason.

As I reflected on it, this is what came:

> It's just another day, I say, a half-smile on my face,
> But this time she sees through that.
> This is what I tell myself.

Is every day the same?
No, it's not…
It's a day harder than most.
It's not the day I lost my little girl,
It's not her birthday,
It's a day we would spend together,
A little differently to other days.

It's a day she would race into my room,
Climb into bed with me,
Gift me with treasures from the school Mother's Day Stall,
Homemade cards and drawings,
These gifts—now like precious gold.

It's a day I stopped to remember why I became a mum.
It's a day I felt appreciated for all those times I didn't.
It was a day of fun, connection and love.

I remember our last Mother's Day together.
You asked me what I wanted to do.
I said I just wanted to stay home with all of you.
We watched movies—all day,
Ate pizza, chocolate and ice cream,
On a mattress in front of the television.
It was perfect.

If I knew this was our last Mother's Day together,
Would I have done it differently?
Definitely not.
That I will be forever grateful for.

I will always be a mum.
I have been a mum longer than I haven't,
It's just part of me.
I couldn't imagine it any other way,
Except for you still being here.

What does Mother's Day feel like for me?
A bittersweet combination of mixed emotions.
The pull of being grateful for what I have and what I had,
The deep pain of not having what I thought I would have,
The knowing that this is how it is meant to be,
The feeling of how messed up it is that it has to be this way.

The smile on my face,
The pain in my heart.

As I go deeper…
The warmth,
The love,
The real smile,
The deep breath.

The depth of my life,
My experiences as a mum.
The person I have become,
The person I am becoming,
The gratitude for everything,
My blessed life.

Being chosen for something I am only just beginning to understand,
Being a mum is only part of who I am.

Reflection Song: I Chose You Mama—Sarah Humphreys with Loren Kate

33

The Time has Come

'It is in the moments of decisions that your destiny is shaped.'
Tony Robbins

June 2019

I was feeling very unsettled. For me, that means sleepless nights, unsettled stomach, headaches and finding it very hard to be in the present moment. Feelings of anxiety and being ungrounded, with my nervous system triggered and heightened, result in emotional instability. This is not a place I like to be in at all and is the total opposite to the environment I'd created for myself over the past few years.

Rob and I had many discussions about the future of his business and the toll it was taking on his health, our relationship, our family and the relationship with himself and other people. He'd been burning the candle at both ends for some time and we both knew some big decisions needed to be made before it was too late. He was exhausted and trying to keep everyone happy—at work, at home, with extended family and friends. This pattern was no longer sustainable. I felt it was just a matter of time until something would happen to change the direction he was heading in, and it scared the hell out of me to think what that could be, especially after everything we'd both already been through. Travelling long hours, always being switched on—he was in survival mode.

We both knew this wasn't how we wanted to live our lives, and I knew for certain we hadn't gone through the pain we'd endured for this to be the outcome.

If there's anything we learnt from losing Ella and other important people in our lives, it's that none of us know when our time is up and life was way too short to be living it that way.

Even though we tried to take time out to go away on weekends or get to the beach (while still being on call), it was just not enough to be able to really relax and feel balanced before having to go back to the same pressures and environments over and over again, each and every week.

It was nothing for Rob to leave home at 4 am and not get home until 10 pm, or even later, and then be on call. He'd been living that way for fifteen years while working for himself, and even longer working for other people.

Through our many conversations, he acknowledged that work had been a coping mechanism for him. After losing his sister and then Ella, work became a great distraction to the pain. Work, like any addiction that takes away pain, even if just for a short period of time, is a clinical condition, characterised by an obsessive and compulsive interest in work. Yet it seems so accepted in society and is often a measure of success, even being looked at and admired for pushing yourself to your limits, working harder and earning more. As a culture, we have come to value growth and productivity, regardless of the negative impacts this has been proven to have on mental health, becoming increasingly detrimental to individuals and families.

There is a long way to go before society changes their outdated opinions and beliefs around work being a crucial tool of growth and performance and starts to consider the wellbeing and health of the worker, both individually and collectively. The only thing we can do is make change at ground level to the way we value ourselves and what we see as being important for our own personal growth as an individual, as a couple and as a family. My hope is that by being a living example of this it may just start to have a ripple effect on those around us, including my two boys.

Work is a place where Rob feels he has great purpose and value. A lot of his needs were being met from giving so much of himself to this part of his life (something that happens to a lot of us). The problems happen when it becomes so unbalanced that we don't know who we are without it, as it has begun to define the person we 'think' we are. When you're stuck in a place that is so familiar and comfortable, it's hard to step out of that, off the treadmill, and into a life you have no idea how you're going to feel about. It's a scary concept, and it takes courage. A lot of courage.

Some nights I lay in bed just praying he'd get home safely when he had to work late into the night on minimal sleep. I'd think to myself *surely God would not be so cruel as to take away someone else I love so deeply, again.*

When he was on the road, Rob always called to let me know if he was going to be late. One night he hadn't, so after hours of waiting, I called him. No answer. I waited half an hour and tried again. Still no answer. I started to panic. I didn't know where he was or what to do. I could feel the fear taking over my body. It was intense. I was trying so hard to stay calm. Half an hour later I called again. Nothing. I was beside myself. It was now early hours of the morning. My body started to shake as I tried to control my mind into not thinking the worst-case scenario. I was walking upstairs to wake Tim, to get him to go with me to look for Rob, when the phone finally rang. It was 2 am. I grabbed the phone, bursting into tears when I heard Rob's voice. He had fallen asleep in his van on the side of the road and hadn't even heard his phone ringing.

I thought I was never going to see him again. This was just one of many nights Rob had to stop to sleep on the side of the road in order to get home in one piece.

Rob had to make the decision about what he wanted to do with his company on his own. That was so important to me and to him. He decided the only way for him to be able to do that with a clear mind and without the influence of others, was to remove himself from all distractions, including work and family. He needed time for his nervous system to settle, time to rest and sleep, to be in nature and connect back to himself on a level where he could connect with his heart and have the clarity to make a decision that felt right for him.

It was time for me to take a step back and trust and allow Rob's process.

I knew in my heart that he already knew, but he needed the space and time to be able to listen to himself and hear it clearly.

A few weeks later I dropped him off at the airport, on his way to a retreat in Queensland. It was a weird feeling for me. We said goodbye with tears in our eyes, knowing that whatever happened over the coming weeks, things would not be the same as they were in that moment.

Driving away, a wave of fear rushed through me. I stopped the car on the side of the road and broke down crying. I couldn't stop. I thought of all the times he'd dropped me at the airport to go on retreat or training and how it must have felt for him. It was so different to be on the other side. We'd have minimal contact for the next two weeks. This was how it had to be, but it was so hard for me, and I knew how scary it was for him as he stepped into the unknown.

I called my best friend and cried down the phone to her. She listened intently, reassuring me that everything was happening just the way it was meant to. I knew this, it was just nice to have someone to reach out to who listened and could hold that space for me. It's all part of letting go. As my emotions settled, I drove myself home.

While he was away, I oversaw the running of the company while managing my client load in my clinic. It was impossible for him to take his work phone away and be able to fully switch off and get the most out of the experience. Thanks to the two amazing employees working for us, we were able to work together to ensure Rob got the break he deserved and had no idea what was going on behind the scenes. It was challenging, but we all survived.

After two weeks I met Rob in Byron Bay, where we booked a little bungalow just out of town to reconnect and give him space to integrate, to process everything that had happened and had been brought into his field of awareness over the past few weeks. I'd also taken Rob's surfboard with me so he could go surfing each day, his meditation.

We were both brought to tears when we saw each other and held each other close. We'd never been apart for that long. His energy had changed so much. We spent the next few days together, hardly leaving each other's side, talking about how we felt and how we wanted our lives to feel as we moved forward from that moment. That time together gave us space—just what we both needed.

He'd made the decision it was time to get out of the industry and sell the business.

I felt like a huge weight had been lifted off our shoulders. Although we had a huge job ahead of us, and it was probably not going to be an easy road, we had a plan and knew what direction we were heading in. For Rob, having to tell others his decision and worrying about disappointing people or letting them down was a huge burden that created a lot of anxiety for him. I understood this was all part of his growth and him being true to himself, living the life he wanted. With each step forward, standing in his truth, the more aligned he would become with his own power and the person he was put on this earth to be.

Often, Rob asked me why I was still with him.

That answer was easy—I saw what he didn't. I saw the beautiful, sensitive, caring, incredible human being he is underneath all the conditioning and programming he'd taken on board to survive throughout his life.

I saw that person and I longed for him to be able to meet himself.

I saw that person and I so desperately wanted to get to know him better.

I saw that person the moment I met him.

I knew that once all the distractions were gone and we gave ourselves the priceless gift of time, the freedom would feel amazing, and we would look back and wonder why we didn't do this sooner.

Knowing in our hearts that everything always happens at the right time.

Reflection Song: Stand By You—Rachel Platten

34

The Show Must Go On

'Perhaps they are not stars but rather openings in heaven, where the love of our lost ones pours through and shines down upon us to let us know they are happy.'
Eskimo Proverb

Rob went back to work as we came up with a plan of how we were going to slowly close the business. I went back to work seeing clients in my clinic. My happy place.

The feeling I get when I'm able to create spaciousness from a place of love for people to be able to move through whatever it is they need to process touches my heart deeply. Everything flows in this space. My mind doesn't need to overthink as I trust each process as it unfolds, knowing the wisdom each body holds within contains the answers people seek. Calmness moves through every cell of my body and stability grounds me. This is a sign for me that I am exactly where I am meant to be.

I feel so indebted to Ella, because I honestly don't know if this is what I would be doing if she was physically still here. While that is extremely hard for me to acknowledge, I believe it is the truth. Part of me feels like she knew I had a higher calling to follow, and this was the gift she gave to me. I know she is always with me, especially in my clinic space, as together we hold people in the healing vibration of love. She had a much higher calling herself, and she could not do this with me from this earthly plain. Ella's passing impacted so many people's lives. The gifts she gave to all who not only knew her personally, but knew of her, had tremendous impact.

One of my clients (I will refer to her as Jane) came to see me after her dog had been viciously attacked and killed by some other dogs who were off their leashes. The dog had been like her baby, such an important part of her family that she felt like she'd lost a child, so she came to me for help processing her grief. Grateful she'd come to see me, I could feel her pain as soon as she walked through the door.

Jane had the ability to connect with people who had passed. It wasn't something she practiced professionally, but it had happened on a couple of occasions, very vividly. We'd had a number of sessions together over the years. One I remember clearly was where Ella came through to her and offered her a beautiful rose—so real it could be smelt. Jane could see her face right in front of her own. That afternoon I walked out into Ella's memorial garden at my house to find an exact replica of that rose. After the rose had bloomed fully, I dried out the petals, put them in a little organza bag and gave them to Jane to keep as a reminder of that moment when Ella had visited her with such a beautiful message of love.

This day, as she lay on my table, I started to clear some blocked energy points on her body, getting her to breathe deeply as her nervous system started to settle and her body became calm. I asked her to visualise her precious dog in a beautiful calm, safe place. Her tears flowed and almost immediately she told me that Ella was there, holding her dog. I could feel Ella in the room as my legs began to tingle (the sign for me that she was definitely with me, which happened regularly).

I knew there was a message she needed to receive from Ella. As we continued, Ella's energy got stronger until Jane felt her energy physically enter her body. She told me it felt like Ella was inside her and had messages for me. This had never happened to her before (or me), but she knew she was in a safe space so decided to allow it to all unfold, letting go of the fear that was initially present. The energy in the room was powerful. After a little while, Jane had to sit up as the intensity of what was unfolding was becoming overwhelming. She asked me to hold her hands. Ella spoke directly to me through Jane as she conveyed every word.

Ella told me that she loved me so much and she was so happy. I told her how much I loved her and missed her dearly. She continued to tell me how beautiful it was where she was and that we would be together again soon. Tomorrow for her was like a lifetime for me. As tears rolled down my cheeks, Jane described in detail the beautiful meadow Ella was standing in and what she was wearing. The messages came quickly, and all Ella wanted to do was hug me and tell me how much she loved me, that she is always with me, sees me and helps me. '*We are a good team, Mum.*' She wanted to make sure I knew that. I certainly did. She reminded me that this was her purpose, as it was mine. Jane told me the feeling of the emotion was so much stronger than the words she was able to express verbally, and she could not put into words the love Ella had for me. She has such a high vibration.

I felt an overwhelming sense of love, peace, hope and promise that life goes on, and that my little girl was in a beautiful place.

Jane could feel it was almost time for Ella to go. As she looked at Ella, she saw her precious dog snuggled securely into Ella's neck. Jane told her it was ok to go and take him with her. She said her goodbyes.

They kept looking back as they crossed a bridge to go into another meadow, her beautiful smile radiant, her blonde hair blowing in the breeze.

As Ella left, Jane's whole body was shaking. Both in tears, we moved outside onto the grass for some time together to process what had just happened and help us both ground ourselves and come back into our own bodies and energy fields.

It was the most incredible experience I've ever had. To this day, it is still hard to put the emotional intensity into words. It was one of those moments in time that you know no one can fully comprehend unless they were there. The energy was so strong it could be felt right through the room and through both our bodies. It was truly amazing.

Jane told me how grateful she was that her dog was now safe with Ella, and if that was why he had to leave this earth then she was ok with that. It had helped her to let go.

Maybe that was his purpose—to be with Ella.

The process helped me just as much as it helped Jane. We both let go and trusted what was happening without any expectations. In doing so, we experienced one of the most incredible moments of our lives. I will never forget that day. I feel so blessed to know Ella is in such a happy, beautiful place. I feel I see this place sometimes in my meditations and I pray that I get to connect with her again soon. I know she is always with me when I'm working in my clinic. Some days, I feel her energy more strongly than others.

Jane is not the only client Ella has come through or shown herself to with messages of love and guidance. I guess she knows when the time is right, and when she sees an opportunity through someone she can channel through, she takes it.

That's my Ella.

When Jane left that day, I went inside and broke down crying. There was so much emotion stored in my body that just had to come out. I rang my mum to share with her what had just unfolded. We were both in tears. She was so happy for me that I got to connect with Ella and so grateful that I had shared the experience with her.

I was very careful who I shared this with, as I didn't want anyone to take anything away from the sacred moment. I believed it was impossible for anyone else to understand the connection and energetic intensity that was felt without being a part of it. However, the more I thought about it as the days moved on, I started to wonder—what if that experience happened to give others hope? What if sharing gave someone the peace and comfort they'd been searching for after losing someone they loved dearly, just to know there is something more out there that is so beautiful. What if I was just the messenger?

I sat with it for some time until it was clear that it was part of my purpose to share the experience with others, knowing in my heart that whoever needed to read it, would.

I wrote about the incredible experience we had and posted in on my social media page, with Jane's permission. I couldn't believe the response I received! I was right. It did exactly as I had thought, connecting people in so many ways, bringing them peace, opening people's hearts and helping them process their own grief.

It gave people hope.

I'm not sure if Ella realises the power she has. Maybe she does. Maybe it's me who doesn't realise the power I have. We are a good team, just like she said. We both have so much to bring to this world.

The next day I woke up feeling a bit heavy, headachy and flat. I went for a walk to try and shift some energy and felt a little better. I could feel this was my body coming back down and trying to find balance after the intensity of the previous day. I was working in my clinic again and wanted to make sure I was grounded and in a good head space.

One of my clients that day was a newer client I'd only seen once before. She'd never seen Ella, and I had no photos of her in my clinic. We weren't that far into her session when she asked if she could share with me what she was seeing. 'Of course,' I told her.

I started to feel energy surging through my whole body, starting in my legs. It felt a bit like pins and needles, but different. Ella was present.

'There is a little girl in a field. She is dancing and laughing and is so happy. She has long blonde hair and blue eyes. Her hair is blowing everywhere. She just keeps giggling. She is wearing a white flowing dress that floats around her.'

I asked her if the little girl had a message for her.

'Yes.'

'It is like part of her joy is inside of me, the joy that I've been searching for, and she is here to show me that it is still there. She is so beautiful.'

She thanked her, and Ella left.

After her session was over, she told me she had felt like she was floating above the bed and didn't feel like she was in her own body at the time Ella came through. She had never experienced anything like it before.

I couldn't believe Ella had come back so soon. Maybe she never left in the first place.

She continues to surprise and amaze me in so many ways.

Reflection Song: In Dreams—Jai-Jagdeesh

35

Reconnection Retreat

'The day you take a step outside of your comfort zone is the day your world will change.'
Steven Aitchison

October 2019

I had just returned from Reconnection Retreat, the women's retreat created and facilitated alongside my fellow Kinesiologist and friend, Tracey. This was something I was deeply passionate about. Holding sacred space for women to come together to connect deeply to themselves and heal touched my soul on such a profound level.

I remember the day, a few years ago now, that I called Tracey. A little nervous, I knew I had to listen and trust my own instincts, following my heart to ask her if she felt it was something she would like to be part of together. As goosebumps covered her body (a sign for her it felt very right), we started our journey together to create something magical. It was a beautiful infusion of energy.

We'd just facilitated our fifth retreat together.

It had been an intense, amazing four days spent with twelve beautiful women, including my mum. This was huge for me and for her. Normally, at the start of each retreat my dad helped me transport everything we needed to our retreat location, including all the food for everyone for the four days we would be together.

Six months earlier, on the morning I was to leave to go to the retreat I was facilitating, I asked my mum if she would like to come along and see where we held these special events. She said she did, and we travelled in the car together.

Something happened for her that day as we drove towards the location, which was only about an hour away from my home, up in the country mountains of the Hunter Valley. Mum started to talk. She talked about her life and told me things she'd never told me before.

Something inside her was starting to unravel.

All I needed to do was hold space and listen.

When we arrived at the retreat, she had a look around and helped me to unpack some food. I asked if she wanted to stay for the retreat. At first, I think she thought I might be joking, but she turned to me and said, 'Next time. I will come next time.'

I was surprised, and part of me wondered if that would actually happen. Committing to go on retreat means allowing yourself to be seen in some way. In order to get the most out of these spaces you need to be prepared to look within, be radically honest with yourself and step into a space of vulnerability, where you have no guarantee of the outcome. Often emotions and feelings that have been buried for long periods of time will have the opportunity to be felt and processed. This was part of healing. This was growth. I wasn't sure if she was ready for that, but I trusted she knew.

It had nothing to do with me. Maybe this was her time. She'd always been a very private lady, keeping things close to her heart, including her own pain, dealing with life and its struggles the best way she knew how, often alone.

To my surprise, as soon as we announced this retreat, she got online and booked herself a place. To say I was a little gob smacked would probably have been an understatement! Two things happened that day in my own body:

1. A sensation in my heart that gave me a warm, loving embrace as I thought about how brave my mum was, making this commitment to herself to step into the unknown—way out of her own comfort zone.
2. An unfamiliar feeling in my gut, as I knew this was a huge moment in both of our lives as we would come together in this circle that was about to be created, like no other I had experienced before. I knew it would bring up a lot of different emotions for both of us.

I wondered what it would be like to be in the same room with such a different dynamic between us. Always mother and daughter. Daughter and mother. Now as retreat facilitator and participant, stepping into two very different roles, as equals. Two brave human souls searching for connection and peace.

This retreat was probably the one that had the most intense energy of them all, from beginning to end. There were a lot of people having huge shifts, processing past trauma and pain they'd held onto for years. Those beautiful women were there to 'do the work' they needed to do for themselves. They were prepared to be seen, to let down their walls so the pain could be released and the love they so longed for, and deserved, could enter their hearts.

As facilitators, we always participated in activities and processes alongside the participants. We shared our own stories and allowed ourselves to feel and be vulnerable just like everyone else. For both of us, this was part of what made our retreats so real. By being real. We knew that every circle of women that came together in our presence was there for so many special reasons, and that the specific group of women, whoever they may be, were meant to be together for that period of time in their lives.

We always trusted the process.

Sometimes that meant there would be certain people in a group who triggered others. While this can be challenging at times, it's all just part of the bigger picture. Being triggered is a beautiful opportunity to learn about ourselves and grow. When you get to the point in your life where you feel gratitude towards the person who is triggering you, that's when you are moving through your pain, the pattern and the story that has been defining you (and often controlling your life). When this happens, you are able to rewrite your own ending.

This retreat would be no different.

As we moved into a few trust exercises, one process was where one person would step into the middle of the circle, close their eyes and start to move their body, while keeping their feet firmly planted on the ground. The other members of the group would form a close circle, supporting the person's body gently as it moved in their direction as they moved back and forward around the circle. When the person finally stopped moving, they would be lifted by the rest of the group, with their eyes remaining closed, and rocked back and forth while being gently lowered to the ground.

This was the same process I had participated in on my first retreat. It can be a lot harder than it sounds, as it involves deep trust and surrendering to allow yourself to be fully supported by others. After half of the group had participated in the process it was my turn. I stepped into the middle of the circle, as I'd done many times before, and when I was lifted by everyone (including my mum) the rocking began. My body began to shake and spasm. It was happening again, similar, but very different to my last KaHuna training experience.

I was fully aware of what was happening as I was lowered to the ground. I looked at my co-facilitator, Tracey, as I said to her, 'It's happening again.' Feeling supported and surrounded by love, I allowed my body to do what it needed to do to shift whatever energy needed shifting.

This was not scary for me, because I trust my body has its own intelligence to know what it needs to do, but for my mum, who was part of this process that she'd never witnessed before, it was terrifying. To see me on the ground, the right side of my body shaking uncontrollably, was too much for her. Her nervous system response was to run, just like she did when she saw me in so much pain when I was in labour with Ella.

She had to move away. So she did.

But she came back. Just like she always did.

She was reassured that I was ok, and was then able to support me as my body settled and shifted into a new state of balance.

I was able to tell her that I was alright and tried to explain that this was just my body's way of releasing trapped emotions and trauma. It can be shocking to see something like this when you've never seen it before or have no understanding of what is going on. Often, our first response can be that there is something physically wrong, but that was not the case. I was fine. My body had just responded to being held by others, as it allowed itself to receive love and be nurtured fully. I believe that my mum being present was an important trigger for me, as I had done this process several times before without my body having that response.

I felt calm and a little exhausted.

After taking time to get some fresh air and ground myself with some wholesome food, I was ready to support others again.

The body has an amazing ability to process what it needs to when it is given time and space. It is incredible what we hold within our bodies, often for so long that it feels like it becomes a new 'normal' way of living.

The power that comes in these moments of self-awareness can be incredibly liberating and freeing.

After a few days on retreat, I saw my mum blossom. Her walls started to come down and I was able to be in the presence of the woman who brought me into this world in a way that I had never fully seen before. Over those days together I witnessed her anxieties and fears, her honesty, her truth and her beautiful heart. I saw her emerge as a different person. She allowed herself to be vulnerable and be seen. She put herself first just by taking the time to be there amongst all those courageous women, which in turn opened her heart to let some pain out and allow love to flow in.

In order for things to change in our lives, we need to do something different. Sometimes this will feel uncomfortable. That's good. That's growth. If we continue to do the same, we will continue to get the same.

I often watched my mum from a distance as she found a quiet place to write, something she hadn't done for a long time. I realised we were not so different after all. This is part of the reason I had to keep writing this book. Not just for me and the people whose hands it would end up in, but for all the women in my family who went before me who had a story to tell, and for whatever reason, never had the opportunity, or took the opportunity, to tell it.

It was such an honour to be able to hold sacred space for all those women, but to be able to do that for the woman who gave birth to me was a true gift I can never share with anyone else. Yet another blessing Ella had given to us both.

In the past, I had offered my mum Kinesiology sessions and KaHuna Massages but she always passed on the opportunity. I knew she was not ready. On retreat, she experienced the gift of a KaHuna massage by my beautiful friend Awen, a woman I trusted deeply who had been a huge part of my own healing KaHuna journey, holding me in spaces of compassion and unconditional love on many occasions as she worked with my body to release some of its trauma and pain.

Mum said it was one of the most beautiful experiences she'd ever had. She went in with an open mind and an open heart and allowed herself to fully receive. My heart smiled to see her bravery in the presence of the unknown. She was trusting, and when we trust our anxiety fades.

When retreat finished, she shared with me how in awe she felt about what I was doing—holding sacred space for women to come together to process and heal. I told her it was just the place I knew I needed to be. When I am in the presence of these women, whoever they may be, I feel I am at home within myself.

She now understood what I did, and why I did it.

I never wanted to leave this world not knowing why I came here in the first place.

I feel so blessed to know, and so honoured to share this space with my mum.

≈

On returning from retreat, I decided it was time to do some more work on myself in relation to my birth and my connection with my mum.

What I discovered was that because I was born six weeks premature not only was I placed in a humidicrib, but I was not strong enough to breastfeed from my mum, so had to be tube fed. I didn't have all the nurturing and contact with my mum that a full-term, healthy baby might have. I learnt very early in life how to adapt, and at times, meet my own needs. My mum was there for every tube feed, but she was not allowed to stay in the hospital with me. Subconsciously, I knew she would come, but I also knew that she would have to leave, and I had no way to get close to her.

Don't get me wrong, I was loved and cared for in every way possible and all my needs were met; however, those first few weeks of my life in this strange world created a belief within me that I had to be strong, resilient, and able to meet my own emotional needs at times.

This is not an unusual thing for premature babies who are taken from their mothers straight after birth. I have no doubt that having developed these qualities helped me become the person I am today and get through some pretty tough situations, but it also made it hard for me to fully receive love from others.

The belief that 'love is hard' started very early for me and was a theme that continued until I was able to recognise it in later life and work through it with my grief counsellor, but only after the loss of my own daughter.

This theme had continued and showed up in my life, time and time again.

Losing my first love to suicide confirmed that 'love was hard'.

Having my first marriage end in divorce confirmed again that 'love was hard'.

Tragically losing my little girl confirmed once again that 'love was hard', along with all the other 'love was hard' stories that made up the tapestry of my life.

That's why, in situations like KaHuna training, where I've attempted to allow myself to fully receive through healing processes, my body wasn't quite sure what to do, so it needed to make some major adjustments. Shaking and spasming are just two ways that my body tries to release, process and adapt to the new experience, to make way for something new, something healthier and gentler. It's similar to the way animals shake and tremble in order to discharge vast amounts of compressed energy after being threatened in some way to dissipate stress. They shake it off and get back to living in the moment.

Sadly, humans have gradually lost this skill of recalibrating their nervous systems. From a young age we have learnt to suppress our emotions, stop our tantrums and often, keep quiet. This repression of our emotional trauma causes it to be stored in our bodies. The response my body was having was a natural, primitive one. The more I allowed my emotions to surface and release, the more my body was able to come back into alignment, the way it was always meant to be. Each time this happened I felt like I was another step closer to coming back home to my true self. My body was just reminding me of what it was capable of when it was given the opportunity to do what it was made to do.

Loving myself enough to uncover the parts of me that want to be felt, observed, released and healed is a beautiful gift.

When humans don't discharge this energy in some way after a traumatic event, we can become victims of trauma. Post Traumatic Stress Disorder (PTSD) develops because of frozen emotions. The energy stays in our bodies and we can develop a fixation on it. This keeps the trauma circuits alive and intact. From there, it can form into a variety of widespread physical symptoms along with anxiety, depression, behavioral and psychosomatic problems. These symptoms are the organism's way of containing undischarged residual energy, keeping us stuck and under the influence of traumatic triggers that can then challenge our ability to return to a state of equilibrium where we can self-regulate once again.

Stepping into spaces where there is support and love to release these emotions has opened up such amazing opportunities for me to have authentic, deep, meaningful relationships with others. I know that when my own pain and trauma is not taking up as much space in my body I have a greater capacity for connection and love to flow freely.

When we are prepared to allow ourselves to be vulnerable and be seen, without fear of judgement or shame, we give ourselves the opportunity to heal. It is in this space that we can start to hear the answers from deep within to the questions we often try to use our logical mind to decipher.

Our bodies are an amazing tool that carry so much wisdom and history, some of which we may never be aware of. Just think of all the generational history that has been passed down through the cells of each and every one of us.

Reflection Song: We Can do Hard Things—Tish Melton

36

What Do You Love?

'It's the simple things in life that are the most extraordinary.'
Paul Coelho

Have you ever thought about what it is you love?

What brings joy and happiness into your life, and the feeling of peace and contentment?

When I stop and feel into what these things are for me, I am reminded how much I have to be grateful for and how blessed my life is.

These are some of the things I love that came straight to me the moment I sat with myself and asked the question:

- The cool dampness of the dew on the morning grass under my feet.
- The sun rising as I sit on my front verandah having my morning cup of chai.
- The sand between my toes.
- My body immersed in water.
- Spending time finding shapes in the clouds—a reminder of the beautiful moments Ella and I spent doing this together.
- The connection that can be created between myself and Rob when we take the time to slow everything down in life and be still.
- Seeing flowers in bloom.

- The smell of fresh herbs, fruit and vegetables.
- Growing my own food.
- Sitting in silence.
- Cooking healthy food in my kitchen to nourish my soul, when it feels like I have all the time in the world.
- Having real, deep and meaningful conversations where there are no limits to what can be discussed.
- Special friendships that flow naturally.
- The warm sun on my face and body.
- Reading a book without feeling I should be doing something else.
- Creating space for people to come together.
- Listening to music.
- Having my family in the one room enjoying a meal together.
- Being able to connect to other people without having to say a word.
- Waterfalls.
- Lying on warm rocks.
- Seeing my boys happy and laughing together.
- Long drives in nature—especially through the rainforest.
- Dancing freely like no one is watching.
- Singing.
- Holding sacred space for others to connect to themselves.
- Being true to myself and living by my values.
- Being spontaneous.
- Feeling motivated and excited.
- The connection I have to my own body and my senses.
- Having a home I can always come back to and feel grounded in.
- Adventure.
- The feeling of freedom.

Try it yourself. You might just be amazed at how many things you come up with. Then make a commitment to yourself to make sure you include at least one of these things in your life every single day.

It's so easy to get caught up in the busyness of life and never stop to be grateful and appreciate the things you have. I remember at the beginning of this journey it was so important for me to find three things every day that I was grateful for, especially on those days I didn't want to face the world or even step out of my own bed.

The fact that I had a roof over my head, could make myself a cup of tea and feel the warmth through my hands as I held it and be surrounded by people who loved and cared about me—some days, these were the only things that kept me going.

I learnt to try and draw the positive aspects from as many situations as I could, even on the days I was hurting so badly. It wasn't easy, and I won't pretend it was. Some days it was possible, and other days it was impossible. I could only see two options—focus on the positive or focus on the negative. Some days I did both. The more I committed to finding the positivity in my life, even if it was in the smallest of things, slowly I was able to direct more of my energy into seeing the good in myself, in the people around me and in the world.

This resulted in me having to separate myself from people whose energy was heavy and negative at times. When I surrounded myself with people who resonated the same energy as I was wanting to attract and emit in my life, I was able to become more positive myself.

Friendships and connections change as you grow. Often, as you let go of people who are no longer good for you, it opens a space for someone else to come into your life who is exactly what you need—a person who vibrates at the same frequency. I experienced this on several occasions as some of my friendship circles changed and shifted dramatically. It's ok for things to change as you grow. Allowing yourself to flow through this change and being open to seeing how everything takes a new shape in life is amazing.

> **Not everyone understands my journey, and I don't see it as my responsibility to explain it to people.**

I am always happy to answer questions from those who are genuinely interested in what I do and why I do it, while navigating through the depths of loss and grief as I continue along this path of what I see as never-ending growth and transformation.

Our lives are a result of the choices we have made along the way and the choices we continue to make each day.

> **We all have a choice. Don't ever forget that.**

Obviously, there are hands we are dealt that we cannot change; however, we do get to choose how we move through those challenges and continue forward in our lives.

If you're not happy with where you are in your life, it might be time to start making different choices.

Reflection Song: Look For The Good—Jason Mraz

37

Conversations

'Connection is why we are here. It is what gives purpose and meaning to our lives.'
                                    Brené Brown

I love having real conversations with people who come from a place of genuine love and compassion and aren't scared to ask the hard questions that so many of us avoid or tiptoe around. I have a friend who exchanges questions with me to contemplate and ponder. We send these back and forth to each other and then come together to talk about it. It's hard sometimes, because it makes you dig really deep into yourself, but it is beautiful.

I've realised throughout my life and the experiences I've had that there are not a lot of people who ask you nothing more than safe, surface questions (as I like to call them), questions that attempt to avoid an emotional response.

I understand this is all a part of getting to know some 'things' about a person, and if that person is probably not someone you're going to see again or spend too much time with, then that may be all you want to share.

What I have found travelling through life was that getting asked the same questions over and over again often became exhausting. It made me wonder how many people really wanted to know me for who I truly was, or more importantly, how I felt.

The more exhausting this became, the more I started to spend time with myself, asking myself deeper questions and resonating with people who did the same.

Connection was, and remains, so important for me.

I knew the connection I had with other people would never be deeper than the one I had with myself, which was why this journey within felt so essential.

Why is it that we don't ask different questions? Deeper questions?

What is it we are afraid of?

The truth?

Or is it that we think there's something we need to do with other people's feelings and emotions that they share with us, but feel ill-equipped to deal with? Some of us have been conditioned to believe it is rude or taboo to ask too many questions, especially personal ones.

The truth is, all we really need to do is listen. *Really listen.* Listen to hear, not to respond or to give our opinion or make judgement. Just give the other person time and space to feel and express their emotions and be 100% present.

Try sitting with someone to get to know them better, without having to talk about yourself.

What would it be like if you met a new person (or someone you already know) and asked them just one of the following questions:

- How are you feeling today? And then really listened to their response, without feeling like you had to respond yourself.
- What would you do with your life if you could do anything at all?

- What brings you happiness?
- What do you do for fun?
- What does creativity look like for you?
- What is the best book you've ever read and why?
- What is the scariest thing you've ever done?
- What is the craziest thing you've ever done and how did it make you feel?
- What is the most incredible place you've ever been to and why was it so incredible?
- What do you value most in life?
- What are some things on your bucket list?
- Do you have any regrets in life?
- At the end of this life, how would you like to be remembered?

When you think of these questions, how many answers would you know about those people you're closest to?

How many would you be able to answer for yourself?

Asking deeper questions creates the opportunity for deeper connections. Why not try it out? You might be surprised at how much more you get to know those you love, changing the dynamics of your relationships.

Pick one person, right now, who you are drawn to having a deeper, more meaningful conversation with, and make it happen.

Some may think that since we've expanded our digital connections we have more opportunities to connect with people. However, the increase in technology and social media has degraded our ability to connect in meaningful ways. Humans are social animals. We need connection to survive and lead a healthy, balanced life. When we connect we thrive and our lives become more meaningful.

Take a moment to think about where it is you need more connection in your life and find ways to fill those spaces if you feel they are empty.

Spend time with the people you love who you can connect with deeply.

Focus on relationships you want to grow that support and nurture you. Ensure you choose wisely, as your time is a precious commodity.

Connect with yourself. Spend time in nature where you can breathe in the fresh air, be free to move and find stillness within. This encourages curiosity and wonder—feelings that inspire more connection in our lives.

Reflection Song: Connection—OneRepublic

38

Rites of Passage

'To be able to love another purely, selflessly, without want or ego, you must first be able to love all of yourself for all that you are.'
Yung Pueblo

Back in Queensland, ready to complete my next level of KaHuna training, I felt sure this level was going to test me. I woke up feeling calm and still, but as everyone started to arrive, I began to feel anxiety rising, even though I knew I was exactly where I needed to be. There were only twelve people on this level, a relatively small group compared to normal. There can be up to twenty-four people on each level at any one time, so even having a group that size was a unique experience.

I realised how different it felt to be in that space, as opposed to the first time, when I attended the women's retreat only a year after losing Ella. I couldn't even mention her name then without breaking down in tears.

How things had changed within me! Now I could talk about my daughter with love and gratitude, knowing in my heart that she was always with me. My energy had changed and shifted so much over the years, little by little, with each healing space I'd chosen to place myself in.

I knew that healing was taking place as I was feeling more peaceful in situations where I used to feel triggered.

**Somewhere along this path as I challenged myself to keep moving forward and face my fears, within it all I had found a place of acceptance.
Acceptance of the things I could not change felt like the biggest lesson I had to learn from losing Ella.**

The unknown of what the week might bring up didn't scare me. I felt open to anything and would allow my body to let me know what it needed to do. Looking inside myself to awaken a little more each time was my purpose in KaHuna training. I trusted the process and I trusted my body.

One of my goals over the days ahead was to be able to understand and release some of the strong attachments I had with certain people in my life. I knew that attachment did not resemble healthy connections in any way, and that this was pivotal to my healing.

Attachments are our own yearning to have things exist in our lives in a very particular way. They can resemble our own inflexibility and fears and can be a product of the pain we have experienced in the past that we have not healed, easily blocking the flow of love that is available to us in our relationships. Pure love invites healing in and let's go of the need for control.

I haven't spent a lot of time on my own over my lifetime. I've been in relationships on and off since I was fifteen years old, was a mum by the age of twenty-one and a wife at twenty-two. At forty-six, I felt like there was an element of attachment in some of my relationships. I understood I was the only one who could work through that and change it so I could start filling my own bucket and be able to give from a much healthier space.

This was no fault of anyone else. This was the life I had created for myself and I took full responsibility for that, yet when I started to self-enquire, I began to wonder what would happen if I believed that these people in my life didn't actually need me at all? What would that feel like? We were all meeting each other's needs at some level. This was a big question for me, and one I hoped I would gain some clarity around over the coming week.

This level of training was pretty intense. As part of it we would be fasting to cleanse our bodies. I was excited—the thought of having my body as a cleansed, clean vessel was a good feeling.

Removing many toxins from my life has had so many benefits, including improving my gut health and immunity, reducing inflammation in my body and my stress levels, while increasing my energy daily. There was a time in the past when I'd get so tired in the afternoons that I could very easily have a sleep every day. Now it's rare for me to feel like that. So, cleansing before going on retreat was not a huge deal for me, although I did notice a difference when I cut out red meat and increased my water intake. Having consciousness about what I put into my body and how it makes me feel is empowering and results in me being fully responsible for myself and my own health.

By lunchtime on day two of the training I hadn't eaten any solid food and I wasn't hungry at all, which was surprising. We hiked to the top of a mountain, where we did a releasing process. My goal was to release the need for attachment. This very quickly brought up feelings of fear and anxiety. My heart started to beat faster, and I felt a heaviness inside my body. I could feel something needed shifting.

We all supported each other through the process. I was invited to stand in the middle of a circle, surrounded by the energy of love and acceptance as tears streamed down my cheeks. Kind words were spoken as each person connected with me by placing their hands on a part of my body. I allowed myself to fully receive the energy of their love. It was a very emotional moment for me.

As the tears continued to fall, it felt like they were falling not from my eyes, but from my soul. They came from the center of my eyes, not from the corners like my tears normally would. I'd never experienced that before.

I felt like everyone's hands were gently holding my heart as it released pain and was filled with love. It was a truly magical moment.

After a while, my body started to shake and twitch a little. I became aware that I was trying to bring my body's natural response under control by disconnecting myself from my emotions. As I moved back into the outer circle, I could feel myself fighting against my own body to try and hold something in.

I wasn't sure what it was, but it wasn't a nice feeling and I started to feel agitated. As we walked back down the hill, I began dry retching. There was definitely something that wanted to get out of my body. All I could feel was fear. My body was shaking again.

One of the facilitators stayed with me and got me to focus on his eyes. I felt confused. Why did this keep happening? There I was, in another space where people wanted to love and support me, and my body was struggling to receive it all. It still felt very foreign.

My body started to settle, but I still felt shaky inside. I couldn't understand why this kept happening.

Was this how my body was now going to process and shift stuck energy and emotions?

I was trying to understand it with my logical mind, instead of just trusting that my body knew what it needed to do and allowing it to fully let go. As I reconnected with my body I started to get a clear message and acknowledge that my fear was attached to losing Rob. For some reason this fear was not attached to anyone else.

Why?

What was it Rob gave me that I was so attached to that I felt I couldn't give to myself?

As I felt into it, it came to me…

Unconditional love.

Rob was the only person in my life that I'd fully allowed in. If he wasn't there for me to receive love from him, what would that mean for me?

It would mean I'd have to love myself. Receiving unconditional love from myself without judgement and not relying on other people to meet this need was what I had to learn to do.

Ok.

I am listening.

I understand.

I have to love all of myself for all that I am.

I could not love anyone else more than this.

Learning to love well was part of healing and it started with me.

Reflection Song: Who You Are—Jessie J

39

Heartbeats

'Take care of your body. It's the only place you have to live.'

Jim Rohn

Here we go again. It was day two still and I'd just gone to bed. My heart was beating out of rhythm. I was contemplating what to do. I didn't want to bring any unnecessary attention to myself, so decided to wait a little while and see what happened. I continued to check my pulse in my wrist, counting beats, 1,2,3...5,6, feeling the gap in rhythm each time as it missed another beat.

I waited.

It stopped and got back into rhythm by itself.

Thank goodness.

I will just go to sleep. I'm sure my body just needs to rest and feel calm. It's been a long day.

As I lay down it started again—back out of rhythm.

Oh my god.

I sat up, feeling frustrated more than anything else, and I waited, checking it by monitoring my pulse.

After a while it went back into its normal rhythm.

I stayed sitting upright, leaned against the wall and closed my eyes. I was so tired. Maybe if I stayed sitting up, I'd be ok?

Just as I felt myself falling asleep, it went out of rhythm again.

What is happening?

I waited a while longer and nothing happened, it was still out of rhythm. I was going to have to let someone know. It wasn't safe to keep going like that.

In 2014, the year we lost Ella, I had to have heart surgery to try and correct the problem, which worked well. Or should I say, had worked well up until that moment. I know when it's out of rhythm because I feel it straight away in the pulse in my neck. I don't even have to touch it. It's a strange feeling. The professor who operated had told me that this type of procedure often only lasts up to five years for some people.

I still remember the day I had the surgery, only four months after Ella passed away. It was a scary day for me. Rob drove me to Sydney and stayed by my side until it was time for me to be taken in to get prepped for the surgery. I was then alone.

What I should have done was ask if he could stay with me, but for some reason I didn't. I'm sure they would have understood. I was trying so hard to be brave. I don't know why. In true 'Kim' style, I didn't ask for help. I was trying to be strong.

I knew my family were terribly worried about me, sitting at home, waiting for the news that everything had gone to plan.

The surgeons were running very late, so I had to wait for a couple of hours in that hospital bed, in a room by myself, trying not to overthink what it was going to be like to be wheeled into an operating theatre. The last time I'd been in a hospital was when I had to walk out and leave my little girl all alone. The last time I'd seen her alive was lying on an operating table in a theatre. I was still having those flashbacks and regularly reliving that day, over and over, in my head.

I felt so alone. It was hard to divert my thoughts from the worst possible scenario when the post-traumatic memories were so prevalent.

I tried to keep myself as calm as possible, focusing on my breathing. I didn't want to go into the operation with a heart that was more stressed than it needed to be. Rob had no idea I was still waiting so long by myself. By the time they came to get me, I just wanted them to knock me out and do what needed to be done so it could be over with.

With a few minor complications during the surgery, it all went well in the end. They blocked the additional pathway in my heart, did some more tests and I was discharged the next day. I hadn't had too many issues since then. Sometimes I'd get a little flutter, like it wanted to go out of rhythm, and I feel it probably would have if it could have, but my understanding was that the pathway was no longer there. I was told at the time that it was not a 100% fix, which was now proving to be correct.

Not the most convenient time for this to happen, but it was happening, and I had to deal with it without putting myself at risk. I finally went to see one of the facilitators to let them know.

I didn't want to have to go to hospital. It was about a one hour's drive away from where we were, but when the facilitators could also feel the irregular rhythm through my pulse and rang the hospital advice line, they were advised to take me in straight away. I was so worried we'd get there and it would go back into rhythm on its own and it would all be a big waste of time, which does happen sometimes, and was usually why I left it longer than I should.

We drove to the hospital, and of course, it went back into what felt like a normal rhythm on the way. We continued to drive so I could get checked over. I needed to take responsibility for my health. The doctors were quite concerned and reminded me how dangerous it was to leave it out of rhythm for too long. I've been spoken to very sternly in the past when doctors have found out I waited twenty minutes before going to hospital.

They found that my potassium levels were low, which could have been a result of fasting, so they gave me a potassium infusion. The pain of the infusion was so intense I had to get them to stop. They monitored me for a few hours, checking everything, and then we were able to go back.

I decided it was probably best for me not to do the full fasting program and went back to drinking fresh juices and eating fruit, including lots of bananas. I remembered that I'd spent some extended time in the sauna that afternoon, which may have also set it off, along with the release of deep emotions. I made a few changes, letting go of some of the higher expectations I had put on myself and took a little step back. It was a good lesson for me to accept that I didn't always have to take the hardest route.

It was time for me to listen more intently to my body. The noise was getting louder.

I knew that the lifespan of the heart surgery I'd had was now up.

Reflection Song: Your Best (feat. Lennon & Maisy)—Nashville Cast

40

Marathon

'Everything happens for a reason—for experience or a lesson. Nothing is ever wasted, because the soul is always gaining insight.'
Leon Brown

Imagine giving and receiving a massage for twelve hours straight throughout the night—giving four massages and receiving four massages, each of ninety minutes duration. This was all part of our training: the KaHuna Massage Marathon.

Drawing on our own Mana (mana being the spiritual energy of power and strength), it was time to dig deep. I felt like this was the moment, on that level of training called 'The Rite of Passage', where I would traverse the summit of my mana mountain.

I felt calm going into the massage marathon. We all participated in a ceremony beforehand which was beautiful and emotional. The feeling of being part of a ritual which represented so much depth, love and connection touched my heart and soul. I felt my heart opening wider once again as we called on our spirit guides to be with us throughout the night.

We walked hand-in-hand to the highest point on the property, overlooking the valley below as we connected our energies through intention and blessings. We chose a sacred name for ourselves during this process. Mine was

Shiva Lingham, the sacred egg-shaped stone that is found exclusively at the bottom of the Narmada River in Western India and represented the balance between individuality and duality, the masculine and feminine within me. It also provided pranic life force energy, which I'd draw on through the night. I felt aligned to the name and place, with the Shiva Lingham crystal underneath my massage table throughout the evening.

We commenced this journey at 7 pm. As we worked our way into the night, I felt empowered, giving and receiving. Before I knew it, it was 1 am and my energy was balanced and stable. I'd been trying not to look at the clock, just allowing it to take place and flow through me.

On the third massage I gave, I felt myself starting to get tired. I wasn't moving my body as fluidly and I started to get a lot of physical pain through my lower and middle back. I was struggling. It was intense.

I managed to finish giving the massage and receive my third massage, hoping that would shift some of the energy for me as I allowed myself to rest and receive for ninety minutes.

I still had one more massage to give and one to receive.

I raced outside for a toilet stop between massages and as the fresh air hit my face, I became extremely emotional and felt overwhelmed.

Why am I pushing myself like this?

My body was hurting and I was exhausted.

Then I felt anger rise within me.

Why am I allowing myself to be pushed? Where did this come from?

It wasn't like anyone was forcing me to do the marathon. It was a choice I'd made for myself, and continued to make.

I started to question *why I am here? What am I trying to prove to myself?*

I was in physical and emotional pain, but I was almost there. Almost at the end.

It is now 4 am—only three hours to go and I was falling apart. Was that what I was there to do? Was this meant to break me?

I'd already had the realisation when my heart went out of rhythm that I needed to stop taking the hardest road, stop pushing myself in all areas of my life, yet there I was, doing it again. Had I not learnt anything?

Once again, I drew on the very last bit of strength and determination I had, pulled myself together and went back into the room to find the next person I was to massage lying on the table face down, waiting for me. With tears streaming down my face, my body and soul hurting badly, I took a deep breath and started to massage. I could hardly move. My knees didn't even want to bend.

I continued slowly, doing the best I could in each moment, telling myself constantly I was almost there.

My back was in agony. *What is wrong with me?*

I managed to finish, but felt terrible because I couldn't give the beautiful body on my table my best. I knew this in my heart, but I also knew it was the best I could do in that moment.

I was angry at myself for not listening to my body when it was screaming at me.

Exhausted, I lay on the table and received my last massage. While receiving, I didn't feel any pain at all. Only when I was giving did I feel the pain.

The sun started to rise and one of my favourite songs played, *Hold My Hand* by Nessie Gomes. A beautiful moment in time that moved my soul and reminded me of what I already knew. I allowed myself to receive her words as her voice floated over and through every cell of my body.

And then it was over.
We were finished.
There was excitement in the room. Everyone was celebrating, but I didn't feel excited.
I did feel relieved.
I also felt disappointed in myself for pushing myself so hard—yet again.
I felt very confused.
I needed to get out of that room.

Reflection Song: Hold My Hand—Nessi Gomes

41

The Morning After

*'Until you cross the bridge of your insecurities,
you can't begin to explore your possibilities.'*
Tim Fargo

After a swim I had some renewed energy and felt a little fresher.

We all went to get some sleep, which was harder than I thought it would be. I thought I'd crash after being awake all night, but my mind had questions that felt like they weren't answered for me.

Three hours sleep. Well, I guess that's better than none.

I awoke, feeling like I'd been hit by a truck. We gathered to have lunch together and I realised I felt like I was out of my body once more. I had a lot of energy in my head, like I was trying to receive some sort of message that couldn't quite get through.

I knew something was stirring.

After lunch, we regrouped to share our experiences of the previous night.

I still felt confused.

And then it came.

As I sat in circle, listening to everyone share their experiences, I felt reluctant to share. Then it was my turn. I took a deep breath and talked about what happened for me during the marathon. My tears fell effortlessly. I had so much emotion stirring within me it was impossible to hold it back. As I talked it through, processing what happened, my body began to shake (again!).

Oh my god, I really don't want this to happen again—not now, I whispered to my body, *please stop, please stop.* But my body was stronger than my mind and I just had to surrender.

I looked at the facilitator sitting next to me, and it was like she had tuned into everything I was thinking and feeling as she looked into my eyes. She gently held me as my body released the built-up energy, shaking and trembling, in front of everyone.

Until there was nothing left.

Finally, it stopped.

I was tired. So tired.

I felt like I couldn't move. I just needed to be still.

It was time.

No matter what else was going on around me, it was time to stop. Time to start really listening and putting myself first.

Time to love myself.

It is ok for me to put my needs first.

They are just as important as everyone else's.

I lay on the floor in a beanbag, exhausted.

All the pain in my body gone.

I was back.

Resting.

I realised the pain in my lower back was the breaking point.

I felt like the camel, and this had been the straw that broke its back. As someone said to me, sometimes the camel's back has to be broken.

The Shiva Lingham crystal was used to help balance the masculine and feminine energy within me, activating my sacral chakra—the root centre of emotions. Too much giving, not enough receiving.

The message was in the pain.

The pain of giving too much of myself hurt so bad, but when I allowed myself to receive, the pain went away, everything softened.

Right there in that space was exactly where I needed to be. Nothing to do. Nothing to give. Nothing to think about. Just allowing myself to rest fully and do nothing. I was wondering why my body hadn't felt better after the first few days on retreat. The fasting and healthy food, the saunas, massages—it just wasn't letting go. It was a beautiful, hard reminder that nothing external will ever take away pain that is coming from within, emotional or physical, until you are brave enough to feel it fully, surrender to it and allow your body to process it, however that presents itself.

It was truly amazing.

I am not afraid of being witnessed, or people seeing my transformation unfold. I believe anyone who is present in those moments is meant to be there for a reason. I have been blessed to have been witness to so many people through their own processes. We heal together. There is no separation. I had no idea what was really happening throughout the process at the time. What I do know now is that I got exactly what I asked for.

I had asked my guides and angels to show me anything I needed to receive to let go of attachments that were not healthy so I could continue to learn, grow, heal and move forward, and that is exactly what they did.

Sometimes we have to go back and repeat old patterns so we can be reminded why we had to change them in the first place. Being able to recognise them in the moment is a gift and huge part of healing with conscious awareness.

Part 2 – The Morning After

I woke in the middle of the night and sat up straight in my bed. My body felt unsettled, like it was shaking on the inside. It shifted quickly. It must have just been some residual energy that needed to move through me. I lay back down and went straight back to sleep.

The next morning, I woke feeling so peaceful. I'd even describe it as a feeling of total serenity. It felt beautiful.

This level of training had reminded me to slow down, love myself, listen more intently to my body and put my own needs first when I need to, even at the risk of disappointing others.

The marathon taught me that I can still give in small doses with love while listening to my body, and when my body is calling out for help, it's ok to stop. My body could never operate effectively in this state. By stopping, I honor myself. I could not continue to give when my bucket was empty, or even half full, for that matter.

To live a life of integrity is to live a life practicing your own values, not just professing them, and integrity itself is one of the values very high on my list. I had to be the example of what I believed in and show up in the world as a reflection of that through each step I was taking, learning along the way.

When I am giving in any area of my life, if emotions or feelings of anger, resentment or sadness arise, then I know it's not the right thing for me to do. Giving should never feel like a chore or obligation. If it does, re-evaluation is needed, checking in to ask what I am doing and why? When I give with an open heart from a place of love, gentleness, and compassion, then I know it is fully aligning with my mind, my body and my soul. This is a beautiful space to be in and a reminder of who I am.

I have learnt so much on the KaHuna journey and I know none of it would have happened if it wasn't for Ella. The emotional pain I suffered from her leaving led me to seek out KaHuna massage for my own healing. The experiences I've had from the people I have received from lit a fire inside me so bright that I just knew I had to be someone who could share this with more people. I believe if I can share this with just one person who has never experienced it before and it opens their hearts to connect deeper to themselves, then this whole journey will have been worth every moment.

KaHuna has brought me opportunities to process and work through my own emotions, feelings, discomfort, and pain, guiding me to grow into the person I am becoming.

There is so much brightness that can come from the darkest of places if you are prepared to feel and heal.

Let the journey continue.

Soul Connection
As shadows start to surface and come into sight,
I feel my body wanting to go into flight.
Today I have a choice, to keep on running away,
Today I have a choice, to allow myself to stay.

Stay in my vision so I can clearly see,
Stay close enough, so I can recognise me.
Acknowledging my purpose with nothing but full trust,
As I allow these shadows to disappear and fall away like dust.

And as they fall and settle into a newfound place,
I clearly see my life here was never a great race.

My body turns to water and begins to flow,
Listening to my heartbeat as my strength starts
to grow.

And every step I take, as each layer unfolds,
The gifts come to the surface, always there for
me to hold.
Hold within my heart,
Hold within my hands.
The day has now arrived when I need no plan.

No need to focus on the past, fear the future
or the now,
No need to try to fix or control, or even know
how.
The stories in my head no longer have a voice,
As I step into my future life,
I create with every choice.

If there is an easy way out,
That is not an option for me,
Determined to discover
Who I was brought here to be.

Kim Cameron

Reflection Song: Sound of Surviving—Nichole Nordeman

42

Re-entry Into the World

'Between stimulus and response there is a space...
In that space is our power to choose our response.
In our response, lies our growth and our freedom.'
Viktor Frankl

I arrived home ready to integrate slowly back into my life once again, hoping the Universe would give me the space to do so gently.

Calling my son Tim from the airport before boarding the plane, as he was picking me up, I discovered he'd had a motorbike accident and was in hospital with a broken rib and a punctured lung. My initial reaction to my children being hurt or at risk is to panic, especially after losing Ella. Tim picked up on that immediately and reminded me it wasn't helpful, which I already knew. Grateful for the reminder, I took a few deep breaths and put things into perspective.

He is alive and is talking to me on the phone.
He is in a hospital and being cared for.
I need to be calm and present for him.
I will do the best I can.

Challenges hold meaning. I wondered what the meaning of this one would be.

Rob was on his way to Sydney airport to pick up Sam, who was flying in from India after being away for a month. Sam had taken himself on a trip through India and

Nepal. This was something he was going to do with Rob and myself in 2017; however, he went on a hiking trip the week before we were meant to depart and broke his arm. He was not allowed to fly in a plaster cast, which was pretty disappointing at the time for all of us. We trusted that this was the way it was meant to be. Rob and I travelled through Nepal for three weeks by ourselves, and Sam was now having an incredible solo experience through India and Nepal making beautiful new connections.

I was picked up from Newcastle airport after what felt like the longest flight ever, and went to the hospital, where they eventually released Tim to go home on painkillers. They didn't have a bed for him and asked us to return the next morning for another x-ray to check the lung puncture and ensure no more air was coming out of his lungs. Surprised they were letting him go home, we monitored him carefully overnight.

The next day, I woke up feeling soft and calm within myself, knowing I needed some time to integrate. Tim was obviously my first concern and priority, but his girlfriend Maddie was with him and took him back to the hospital to have his x-ray. Rob was going into the workshop for the day, and I knew he'd probably like me to be with him, but I also knew this was a time where I'd be tested to put my needs first, as hard as it was. It was challenging but empowering at the same time to be feeling into what I needed and to actually follow through.

Being honest with myself and speaking my truth, I let Rob know I needed some time at home alone. He was understanding. He knew what it was like to come home after being away on a retreat.

I checked in with Tim to see if he needed me to go with him. He didn't. I asked Maddie to call me once they had the x-ray results and reminded her I would only be ten minutes away. It might only seem like a small thing to do, but it was a big step for me, and it was important for them as a young couple to have the space to support each other. They knew where I was and that I'd always be there for them if they needed me.

Taking a step back allows others to take a step forward.

Later that day, I had to transfer Tim to the John Hunter Hospital. After having to go through triage for the third time in two days, they gave him more painkillers and told him to go out in the waiting room and wait. I was starting to wonder why they even asked us to go there in the first place. He was in so much pain, trying to lie down over a couple of plastic waiting room chairs with a broken rib and punctured lung. We waited for hours, well into the middle of the night. We were told when we left our local hospital that everything had been arranged for Tim to be admitted and monitored, but there was just confusion and no beds.

Not one of our favourite places to be hanging out in, neither of us wanted to be there for more reasons than one. This was the emergency department Ella was rushed into five years earlier. We did our best to stay focused on the present situation, but there were many reminders and triggers all around us.

They finally had a bed for Tim in Emergency at 4 am and monitored him as I put my head on the bottom of his bed to try and get a few moments of rest. We were both exhausted. They came to get him shortly after and wheeled his bed to the ward where he was to be admitted, I went to get him some food. He hadn't eaten since lunchtime the day before. Not long after I got back, a doctor arrived and told us he was going home.

What?

After obvious differences in opinion and miscommunication between doctors, we took Tim home for four weeks of rest and recovery. No lifting anything over five kilos in weight, which meant no work. That was going to drive this active young man a little crazy. We took him home and settled him in for his recovery.

I was going back to work the next day. My clinic was at home, so I was able to keep an eye on Tim between clients. I felt like I hadn't really had enough time to process what transpired on retreat and integrate back into my life at home. I knew how important this was, so I would just take things slowly and mindfully and try to maintain a feeling of balance and connection with myself.

Being able to step back into everyday life with awareness was part of the process.

As Sunday morning rolled around, I felt very sad and started to cry. I didn't know why, but I couldn't stop, so I just went with it. I was tired and needed sleep, so I listened to my body and did exactly that.

Today is for resting and sleeping.

I knew all I had to do was slow down and honour myself. I was listening.

Reflecting on the meaning of why I was faced with this immediate challenge after undergoing such a huge personal transition, I realised it was a timely reminder of being aware of my own reaction or response in a time of crisis or an event that brought up past fears. It gave me the opportunity to change my own reaction in the moment to change the pattern, as I took a step back and trusted that other people in my life who I loved so much were capable and responsible for themselves.

They were no longer children, but young adults, navigating their own way through the world. I didn't always need to be there; I just had to love them and know in my heart that they knew where to come if they needed me. This didn't mean I had to be available every second of every day. This was all part of detaching, letting go and finding comfort in not needing to be needed by others.

I knew this was part of their growth as well as mine. Being conscious in each moment of how I am responding or reacting to life is key to being able to change ingrained patterns and conditioning. The more I practice this the more I am able to witness myself. It doesn't mean I get it right all the time, but it does mean I get to acknowledge my own behaviour and choose a different response next time if it does not align with how I want to show up in the world.

This to me is a huge part of taking full responsibility for myself.

Reflection Song: Be Slow—Harrison Storm

43

Full Moon

'You can choose courage, or you can choose comfort, but you cannot choose both.'
Brené Brown

I often get messages so clear and precise they cannot be ignored. They usually come in the very early hours of the morning, keeping me awake. I try so hard to get back to sleep, but it's pointless. Eventually, I feel like the only choice I have is to get out of bed, get a journal and start to write and see what comes through. Clarity is so prevalent in those moments.

This night was like no other in relation to how clear the messages were.

I was shown an image of a meditation being held at my home. The centerpiece was Ella's patchwork quilt made from pieces of her clothes, one of my most treasured possessions and certainly not something I share with everyone. Yet I felt I couldn't question the vision and trusted that this was what I needed to do. I continued to write.

I held regular meditation evenings at my home, usually on the Full Moon or New Moon, often with anywhere from ten to twenty people in attendance. This was something I loved to do. We had a beautiful space to share, which sat on one acre, overlooking a mountain range. Being able to bring people together into this peaceful energy to experience the moon rising over the trees was magical.

I had a feeling deep within me that this was going to be an extra special event. I was right.

Almost forty people joined me that evening for the meditation, including my mum and dad. My dad had never been to anything like this before, but I'd been sent a message to contact him and ask him to be there, so I did.

I trusted every step of the process. Rob served fresh chai to everyone as they arrived, and we had an area for people to mingle and meet while my friend played and sang songs on her guitar from our back verandah before we started. I had the grass area set out with Ella's beautiful quilt as the centerpiece, surrounded by crystals, flowers, sound bowls and oracle cards. I could feel the magic building even as I was setting up the space.

I led the evening with words, music, song and meditation as hearts gently opened, tears fell, emotions were felt and expressed, connections were made, voices were heard, and energy shifted.

As I sat in silence, I invited people to place their hands on a small piece of Ella's clothing on her quilt that they were drawn to and feel into what it was they needed to let go of that was weighing them down. As people rose from their seats, one by one, and moved towards Ella's quilt, a feeling of overwhelming gratitude and love washed through me.

Each person voiced what they wanted to let go of (silently or aloud) on the rising of the full moon as we entered the new decade of 2020, trusting that all would be released through the beautiful processes of the night into the Universe, being taken care of exactly as it was meant to be. I felt Ella's presence so very close, along with all the other beautiful angels that had been called in to be with us in the incredible circle of love and healing.

Then my dad got up and moved towards the quilt. He got down on his hands and knees and leant over to a piece of her school uniform, gently placing his hands on it with so much love as tears fell down his cheeks and mine. I could feel the depth of his pain as he reconnected with what he had lost and was grieving for so deeply. I felt his heart break open and become a little lighter. It was a moment in time I don't think either of us will ever forget. It was raw and it was beautiful.

I am so glad I trusted my senses enough to ask him to be there and that he trusted himself enough to step out of his own comfort zone to come along, not knowing what to expect. In my eyes, this is one of the bravest things we can do as humans. I see it in everyone who is courageous enough to step into spaces and feel the vulnerability as they show up and allow themselves to be seen.

Creating these spaces is my passion. I know how much everything changes when this step is taken. I have experienced it time and time again. It is what drives me to continue learning about myself each and every day and motivates me to keep stepping into these environments where I am giving myself the opportunity to feel everything. Allowing myself to be seen, in a way that not everyone sees me, letting go of the stories that hold me back so I can show up in the world as the most authentic version of myself, learning every step of the way.

For so many years, I pushed my feelings under the carpet to keep the peace, even if this meant I was doing something that didn't feel right for me. I didn't stand up for myself because I felt powerless and unworthy. If I did stand up for myself it came out as defensive, resentful anger that had never been given the space to be processed for what it really was. I gave in to my external circumstances and situations at times and allowed them to control my life and did not take responsibility for myself and my own healing.

This type of living came from deep, suppressed pain and I knew I was the only one who could process and heal those parts of myself that were hurting.

Making that conscious decision and taking action to find ways that could support me through this as I stepped through my own fear, judgement and grief changed my life and I was now seeing how it was now changing the lives of those around me.

> **It was never just about me.**
> **As the connection to myself grew stronger and healing gradually took place, I could hear and see clearly what I needed to do, not just for myself but for those around me that I loved.**
> **I could feel the healthier vibration that was now moving through me and being sent out into the world and it was so beautiful and peaceful.**

At the end of the evening, a lady came up to me to let me know that one of the songs I'd been called to play during the meditation was a song her sixteen-year-old daughter danced to in her concert recently. It had brought her to tears.

Her daughter's name was Ella.

Messages had come through loud and clear from the moment the idea of this gathering was sent to me. Thank you, Ella, for yet another reminder that you are always around.

My heart was overflowing. I felt deeply connected to every single person there on that beautiful night. I know this moment in time will live on in the hearts of all who were present.

The gift of Ella's life keeps giving, by bringing people together to heal. As she continues her mission through me, I will continue to be open to hear and trust every message she sends.

This is what it is all about.

Reflection Song: A Hundred Thousand Angels—Bliss

44

Five Minutes More

'Time is free, but it is priceless. You can't own it, but you can use it. You can't keep it, but you can spend it. Once you've lost it you can never get it back.'

Harvey Mackay

Another question finds its way into my world when I am asked what I would do if I had 'Five Minutes More with Ella'.

I thought about it, and this is what came…

> I would hold you so close, so you could never leave.
> I would laugh with you and make silly faces.
> We would dance and sing like no one is watching.
> And if they were, we would not care.
> We would make funny videos and eat as much ice cream as we could.
> We would watch the clouds above and see what we could find.
> We would jump on the trampoline.
> Swim in the pool—doing summersaults underwater.

> We would talk and play games like there was nothing else in the world to do.

Then I went a little deeper, the next layer below the surface and felt into the depths of my heart.
What would I do with Five Minutes More with you, my beautiful girl?

> I would lie with you, holding you gently, yet so tight in my arms, dreaming that this is how it would always be as I feel my heart beating against your back and your little heartbeat in my hand.
> I would smell your beautiful soft hair.
> No words to be said, feeling nothing but peace as a soft smile moves across my face, knowing we are here in this moment, together.
> With nothing to do.
> Nowhere to be.
> Just you and me.
> Feeling forever blessed that I was given the chance to hold you in the first place.
> Eternally grateful for the gift of you.

That is what I would do with Five Minutes More. And from that moment of reflection, this comes.

> **Five Minutes More**
> Five minutes more is never enough.
> Why would we wait until it's too late?
> The people we love the most,
> Are the ones who are here.
> When are we fully present to hold those ones near?

Sometimes we forget,
Sometimes we get lost,
In the things that don't matter, that come at a cost.
And none of us know just how long we are here,
We only get this day, don't live it in fear.

Open your heart,
Connect to your soul,
Connect to those people you are longing to hold.
Let down all those walls,
And just let it flow,
There's no time to hold back,
Just let it all go.

There is no guidebook,
We don't know the plan,
No map is provided,
We only get one chance.
One chance to choose how each day will be,
Not for anyone else,
Only for me.

How do I want
To remember this time?
When I look back at each day of my life,
Did it all matter?
Oh, what I would do,
To have five minutes more to spend it with you.

Time that has passed,
I can never get back.

Part 2 – Five Minutes More

And I think of the things,
That we would do,
If I had five minutes more,
To spend it with you.

And when all of this stuff,
Moves out of the way,
I would hold you so close,
And pray you could stay.

But I know in my heart,
This power's not mine.
And when it is time,
Our lives will entwine,
Forever in love and moments so dear,
Never to part.
Why am I the one that's still here?

But I will be grateful for all of the time,
For each little memory,
For every smile.
For the giggles and laughs,
The tantrums and tears,
The kisses and hugs,
Precious moments held dear.

For the gifts that you gave me,
And continue to give,
For every five minutes,
That I get to live.

So, what would you do,
With five minutes more?

Feel into your heart,
Reach down to your core.

Who would you be with?
What would you say?
What would you do?
If this was your last day.
                Kim Cameron

Reflection Song: Carry You—Missy Higgins

45

December

'If you want something you have never had, you have to do something you have never done.'
                                        Thomas Jefferson

December 2019

We continued to work towards closing Rob's company down. I worked in my clinic three days a week and at Rob's workshop the rest of the time, helping with the administration and day-to-day running of everything. Emotions were high, and things were quite tense between us at times. It was a stressful time in our lives.

It wasn't really where I wanted to be, but I knew we had to work together to make it happen. Rob still needed to work onsite to keep the business side of things operating until we actually closed, and I was left to manage the rest. He still worked long hours and I was worried about his mental and physical health. Even though we'd made the decision, there was such a huge process to go through to make it happen. It wasn't something we wanted to just close the doors on. Rob felt very strongly about finishing what he'd started in a manner that aligned with his values and the high expectations he'd always put on himself, which I totally understood. The problem was, there would be no end to it until we announced the closure and everyone was aware of what was happening and was on the same page, or at least reading out of the same book as us.

The phone kept on ringing constantly, the work kept coming and Rob kept pushing himself to his absolute limit. I didn't think he could put any more into the business than he already had over the past fifteen years, but it felt like he was working even harder to compensate for the fact that he'd made the decision to close. The feeling of letting other people down in order to take care of himself was a difficult place for him to be in and I could see the struggle was tortuous. Some days, it felt like there was no end in sight and I wondered if I was just enabling him to keep going at that pace. I'd go into the office and sort things into manageable chaos so he could continue on a path that was clearly wearing him down to the bone. It felt like we were still hamsters on a wheel, but now the wheel was spinning faster than ever.

Both operating from a level of survival in that space, our nervous systems were triggered. The stress and responsibility we took on in that environment was dangerously unhealthy. One day I just had to walk out before I exploded. I walked around the block a few times, breathing deeply, before going back in a little calmer. Rob told me to go home. He hated it when I felt like that. I knew he felt guilty that we were in that place, and that I was in a space I didn't want to be, but the only way we were going to get through it was together, so I stayed. We just needed to know when to take time out for ourselves before we hit breaking point.

We continued to do what we needed to, trying so hard to focus on the bigger picture of what things would be like once this part of our journey had some closure. This was just one of the many moments of imbalance, frustration and at times, despair, that we experienced.

Part 2 – December

Our plan was to give all customers six months' notice. This would enable Rob to feel comfortable he had enough time to transition people over to other companies and feel good about walking away, knowing he'd done everything he possibly could. Rob is a person who usually goes above and beyond in everything he does, so I knew this was something he'd need time to do. I did my best to be as patient as I could.

I knew this was one of the biggest lessons I had to learn from Rob—patience.

We had six months to get through until it would all be over. I hoped we'd make it. We were already exhausted; no way could we continue to live our lives like that. My worst fear was him having an accident travelling to and from work because he was so fatigued, his life being over before he had the opportunity to enjoy what he'd worked so hard for—before our life and dreams had the chance to become reality.

We'd already been through so much together and worked hard to set ourselves up for our future, but in reality, we knew life could be taken away from us in a split second.

Taking a step back to evaluate our lives and making commitments to ourselves that not everyone else understood meant we were starting to put ourselves first. The changes we were making would not only change our lives, but the lives of those around us, and that could only have a positive flow-on effect.

I'm not the type of person to not follow through with my intentions and goals. I like less words and more action. If there was something I wanted to do and I believed it could be done, then I'd get in and give it my best shot. Sometimes it would work out better than I expected, sometimes not, but each time I stepped out of my comfort zone, I knew that I was growing. I was always looking for ways to move forward and expand myself, creating opportunities for people to come together or making memories with those I love. I knew in my heart Rob and I had many more memories to make together in this lifetime.

Regret is described as a feeling of sadness, repentance, or disappointment over something you have not done or failed to do. This is not something I am prepared to feel when it's time for me to leave this world. So, I put things in place to ensure that will not be the case, because this is something I can create.

My past has given me the most incredible opportunities to grow and to learn so much about myself, others and the world, and I am grateful every single day that I get to wake up and experience this life, in all its beauty, with all its challenges.

I had a lot of hope and believed in my heart we could wind the company up together and come out stronger on the other side. It was just another part of our journey to becoming the people we were both longing to connect to, personally within ourselves and with each other.

There are so many reasons we were brought together in this lifetime. Holding on to the two strongest messages we received from Ella, 'Just Do It,' and, 'You should get yourself home from work earlier,' gave us a strong reason to follow the path and create a more balanced life.

It was a short-term goal compared to our life so far, yet it involved such a huge shift in our consciousness and awareness of what was important to both of us as we made this dream a reality.

Envisaging our future with hope helped to make the situation more bearable. Believing good things would happen and having faith in something much bigger than myself motivated me to continue to take the steps needed to make this happen.

So many moments in our lives can be created into lasting memories, but it's not until those moments become memories that we realise their precious value, and often when it's too late.

One of our dreams was to travel around Australia in our caravan. This was our goal once we no longer had the business. We knew it would be a great way to have the time and space we needed to reset and process not only the last fourteen years of our life together, but our whole lives, as we created space for deep connection.

Christmas 2019 was very different for us. Tim and Maddie had to leave home early to see Maddie's family and Sam was no longer living at home, so he wasn't with us either. For the first time ever, it was just Rob and I on Christmas morning. Such a weird feeling. As we sat on our verandah drinking cups of chai tea and watching the sun rise, it was very peaceful and quiet, but it also made me think about what it would be like when we had none of our children living with us anymore. It was a strange concept for me. I'd been a mother since I was twenty-one years old—more than half my life. There were so many changes yet to come, all part of our evolving life cycle.

Throughout the day we saw all our families, which was lovely.

I'd decided I didn't want to give people 'stuff'. I wanted to give as many people as I could experiences that would create memories. So, I bought Rob and I tickets to fly to Alice Springs to visit Uluru and Kings Canyon in February, a quick adventure and a much-needed mini break to keep us going until the business was closed down.

We booked accommodation to take the kids to Bondi Beach for a weekend in January, staying in an apartment overlooking the beach. I gave my niece and nephew a voucher to spend the day with me at an adventure park, and I bought tickets to take my mum to see the Ballet.

Creating memories is so important, and this way I could spend time with those I love and do just that.

I wondered what 2020 would bring for us. I wasn't sure I could even imagine the change we were about to experience.

Reflection Song: Never Giving Up—Fearless Soul

46

Home Retreat

*'Let there be spaces in your togetherness,
And let the winds of the heavens dance between you.
Love one another, but make not a bond of love.
Let it rather be a moving sea between the
shores of your souls.
Fill each other's cup,
But drink not from one cup.'*
Kahlil Gibran

Rob and I had been working with a Holistic Counsellor to help us get through the challenges we'd been facing during the transition of closing the business and the changes taking place in our lives. In all honesty, they weren't new issues, just ones we needed to spend more time working through together to create the life we desired.

I feel it is really important to reach out and access support when you need it. The first step to creating change is being able to acknowledge that you need help. To have someone who is able to be unbiased and look at things from a different perspective can often feel like someone has turned on the light switch.

Usually, the stories we tell ourselves, that we create around problems and issues, are based on past wounds and trauma we've never processed or addressed. Our bodies become a storage facility for the emotions that have never been given the space to complete their full energy cycle.

We carry those unhealed wounds from one relationship to the next. And then, we meet the person who is our mirror (and often our greatest trigger), who comes into our lives to help us to see ourselves more clearly, often opening our eyes to a reality we've tried to avoid or deny. This is a true gift if you can look into this without your own mask on.

Not always an easy task.

Rob and I are both committed to working together to create our best life possible.

> **Finding a partner in life who is willing and open to looking within themselves and prepared to do the work individually and as a couple is a blessing.**

This type of relationship can feel more difficult at times, but it can also be the most rewarding. As we both continue to work on ourselves to develop our own emotional maturity, we become partners in healing with a greater capacity to see and hear each other from a place of love, supporting each other the best way we can in the creation of our own happiness.

We'd been on a couple of retreats together over the past few years that had changed our lives in so many ways. Each one offered unique opportunities for incredible growth and healing for the both of us. We decided instead of spending money going on another retreat together, we'd create our own three-day retreat at home, just for the two of us. We had a beautiful space, all the tools we could possibly need, and we had each other. After Christmas we let those around us know that's what we were doing so they could respect our space and made a commitment to each other to spend those three days together at home, alone.

It was an interesting exercise. I tried to let go of all expectations but was also hoping we could create some depth in that space together. Part of creating a retreat at home was to help us to learn to relax in our own environment, without focusing on all the jobs we'd like to get done that surrounded us and would normally be getting our attention and keeping us busy.

I believe this felt easier for me as I'd spent more time at home, working from my clinic space, and was able to have breaks during the day where I could take time out to sit and appreciate the beauty that surrounded me. For Rob it was a bit more challenging. Leaving home before the sun came up and getting home in the dark meant that on weekends he was often only able to see and focus on the work that had to be done around the place.

We would go away regularly just to give him the opportunity to relax, which felt crazy when we had such a beautiful space at home. When we brought our house, we both said it was a place we would pay to go on holidays to, and now we get to live here every day of our lives. Yet we still hadn't really had time to enjoy it together—three years on!

For three days, we slowed everything down. We took time to prepare meals, have cups of tea and coffee on the verandah together, sat by the pool, swam, read, did some yoga and meditation, rested and slept. It was very relaxing.

As with most retreats, when you give yourself the time and space to sit in the silence you start to feel. Things start to process because they now have the space to do so. When we take away all the things we normally use to distract ourselves, we are then able to start to connect and feel what is really happening for us under the surface, patiently waiting for the opportunity to be felt. It can feel a little confusing as you start to experience the different sensations of suppressed emotions rising in your body.

Recognising that was happening, we created opportunities for each other to express how we were feeling and tried to hold each other in that space with love and understanding. When we felt we did not have the capacity to hold that space for each other anymore, we took time out alone to be with ourselves.

We wrote letters to each other and exchanged them, working through our feelings in the best way we knew how in the moment. It was not always pretty. Anyone who thinks facing suppressed emotions that have often been pushed down into our bodies for many years is easy is mistaken; however, I knew our awareness was developing and our reactiveness was becoming less and less and I trusted that everything was unfolding exactly how it was meant to.

I have found that writing is a great tool to help process my emotions and feelings before sharing them with others, especially when it feels turbulent and confusing. Writing has been crucial to my growth and personal development throughout my whole life, helping me to understand myself on a deeper level and be able to express myself more authentically in the world.

We should never try to drag others into our own emotional turmoil. Sometimes taking time out to find stillness, in whatever form that resonates for you, is the healthiest thing to do for everyone.

Many times in the past, Rob and I faced challenges that were never addressed and resolved, usually because we either didn't have the capacity to deal with them, were 'too busy' and did not make them a priority, or it simply felt too hard. The problem with that was the issue never actually went away, it just became invisible on the outside, while the emotional pain could still be felt on the inside.

As our three days continued, we moved through many different emotions and feelings, always finding ways to come back together and reconnect, sometimes in the smallest of ways.

A smile.
The touch of a hand.
An offer of help.
A kiss.
A hug.
A cup of tea.
A massage.
The sharing of a fun memory.

Remembering everything we had been through to get to where we now were.

Sometimes it can be the simplest of things that create the greatest connections.

Being open and honest in relationships can be hard at times when there is unprocessed emotions and trauma. Often in life, we haven't even invested time into discovering what our own true values are, let alone discussed them with the person we've chosen to spend the rest of our lives with and then make decisions aligned with those values.

There is no way we can have meaningful relationships without knowing what our own values are and living our lives in reflection of those values.

It is important when we are discovering what our own personal values are to check in to ask ourselves if they are actually our values, or the values of those who brought us up and have been strong influences in our lives. This can have a huge impact on what we think is important to us.

So there we were, being brave and vulnerable, doing the work we felt we needed for our relationship to continue to flourish and grow, for us to live a life that aligned with our values and what was important for us. It wasn't easy, but for me it was a lot easier than living in a relationship where the same issues kept coming up over and over again. Life is way too short to be living in that space, and if that meant I had to continue to honour myself and step forward, even when I wanted to step backwards, that was what I would do.

Why?

Because I am important enough to do that for and I wanted meaningful relationships based on deep connection in my life.

Our three days together at home, focusing on our relationship and ourselves, was a beautiful experience that brought its own challenges that we were both grateful for. Making the commitment to ourselves and following through with it was essential in making this a priority in our lives.

I felt sure our retreat at home was the first of many spaces we would create in honour of ourselves and our relationship. It's not something we can just take for granted—our marriage, that is. If we don't allocate time to prioritise our relationship, our connection can diminish very quickly. Like all relationships with the people in our lives, you cannot just neglect them and expect to still have strong, meaningful connections.

One of the greatest investments you'll ever make is in the time you put into the relationships that have meaning for you and nourish your heart and soul.

Often, I reflect on couples I've worked with, and even myself throughout my own relationships, and think, *this is the person you have chosen to be with, yet this can also be the person you take for granted and treat the worst at times.* I know this is not the case for everyone, but I have seen and heard it so often and experienced it myself.

**Make time to connect with those you love.
Relationships don't just happen.**

Rob and I will continue to work on ours for the rest of our lives, because it is important to us. We know it will change over time as we go through different seasons in our lives, but we know we will always be there to love and support each other as we discover ourselves as individuals and come together to form a stronger connection that always provides an environment for growth, understanding and compassion.

**Great relationships are not great because
they have no problems.
They are great because two people have
come together and care enough about
each other to support the growth of each
individual, which in turn strengthens their
connection with each other.**

Everyone deserves happiness in their lives. When it feels out of reach, check in with yourself to see if your heart is open and if the energy you're putting out in the world and into your relationships is the energy you want to receive back. If it isn't, change it.

Be open and honest, even if that means stepping out of your comfort zone and having the hard conversations.

Often, these are the conversations that contain our suppressed feelings and emotions that keep us feeling stuck. Feel the fear and do it anyway, for this can be the gateway to your freedom.

Listen to what you need.
Find your voice and ask for it.
Don't be afraid to be seen and heard.

Reflection Song: Brave—Sara Bareilles

47

Time Off

'Self-care is not self-indulgence, it is self-preservation.'
Audre Lorde

Months went by and I had fallen back into my old pattern of giving way too much of myself to everyone and realised I needed some time off. I needed some time out of my clinic and out of Rob's workshop. Having that awareness, even when I had stepped back into the old pattern, was a huge part of my growth.

I'd talked to Rob and told him I needed to take a couple of weeks off, but it was still challenging for me to be strong enough to see it through, as I always felt like I was letting others down. I had clients who wanted appointments. I was trying to do everything I could to assist in the running and upcoming closure of the company, and Rob was still working long hours himself. I knew if I continued to work at the capacity I was, I'd be no good to anyone. So, I was listening to what I needed and doing my best to follow through with it. I knew that each time I changed this pattern, I was making myself a priority in my life.

I had to. I couldn't keep splitting myself in two—trying to run my clinic and be in a space I love so much, where I felt balanced and at peace, then racing to the workshop to be immersed in a stressful environment that filled me with anxiety.

I was also trying to fit more clients into the reduced amount of days I was in my clinic, which I knew was not sustainable for me.

My body ached and I was experiencing migraine headaches—not a good sign. I had to listen to my body. I could sense my migraines were related to the pressure I was feeling, along with the need to try and keep things that were happening around me under control in order to get to our end goal. There was a lot of anxiety, stress and seriousness present and very little joy. I knew I hadn't been listening to my intuition and was ignoring my own needs, and that's never a good combination. It was all feeling a little crazy and out of control. We were getting closer to our goal of closing down the business, but there still seemed to be so much to do and it was overwhelming for both of us.

I took the time off to rest and reset so I'd have enough energy to continue. With both of us feeling high levels of stress, neither could support the other. I knew I was unable to support Rob emotionally and resourcefully from the place I was in.

No-one will ever treat you better than you treat yourself.

I'm so grateful I listened to what I needed and took action, not pushing myself way beyond my capacity. It was all part of breaking the cycle of old habits and conditioning that no longer served me in any way.

I knew if I continued to do what I had always done, I would continue to get what I had always gotten.

I had to trust myself and listen to my body once more.

I knew it held the answers.

Reflection Song: A Reminder (Remix)—Trevor Hall

48

Reflecting in Nature

*'I go to nature to be soothed and healed, and to
have my senses put in order.'*
John Burroughs

We were heading out for the weekend to a community retreat a friend was running, an event where we'd be surrounded by likeminded people expressing themselves through music, art and dance, sitting together in nature, moving, creating, listening, talking and sharing food.

What a great way for us to re-centre ourselves in the midst of what felt like our own little crazy world, and so nice to be around authentic people who weren't interested in what you 'do' or what you 'have', but in how you feel and what makes your soul sing. It was a beautiful weekend, with the opportunity to do yoga, nature and bush craft, massage, dance and sing.

I spent some time alone in nature, on an incredible piece of land in the middle of the bush, and this poem flowed through me.

> **Then There Is This**
> Stopping in silence,
> Reflecting in song.
> Creating with hands,
> It's been so long.

Pushing for deadlines,
Expectations so high.
Trying to please,
A life no longer mine.

Confusion about
How it all got this way,
It all seems so simple,
Yet so hard to say.

This life I am living,
I'm not sure whose it is.
All these things that surround me,
Whose dream is this?

And then there is this,
Community and love.
No one comparing,
Just rising above.

Above all the garbage,
We hold in our head,
Destroying our peace,
Digging our own death bed.

The birds they sing sweetly,
The breeze feels so fresh.
The gentlest of raindrops,
A space just to rest.

The trees whisper softly,
Such wisdom and strength.

> I ask them a question,
> They answer—at no length.
>
> Clear as the blue sky,
> What I knew all along.
> If only I had stopped sooner,
> To hear this beautiful song.
>   Kim Cameron

Nature invites me into the deepest places within myself where a natural connection takes place. It is in this place that I remember why I am here and am reminded of everything I already know.

While a weekend never seems like long enough, sometimes it is just enough to keep following the direction of my own heart and soul.

Reflection Song: Rooted—Aisha Badru

49

Within the Busyness

'Surrender is the simple yet profound wisdom of yielding to rather than opposing the flow of life.'
Eckhart Tolle

After waiting almost two months for our interested buyer to come back to us with a definite answer about purchasing the business, they pulled out of the negotiations. I was crushed. I realised I'd been so attached to the sale going forward that I hadn't prepared myself for it to go the other way. I had looked at the sale as our ticket out. I felt we had so much riding on it.

Defeated, I couldn't stop the tears. I cried and cried until there was nothing left. I felt so much for Rob. He'd worked his ass off to get the business to where it was, but because Rob was what made it so valuable, no one wanted to give it the value it deserved unless he agreed to work for them for years into the future. This was not something he was prepared to do. Not an option. He wanted out.

I felt so stuck and questioned why it was happening that way. I tried so hard to stay positive and remind myself there would be a reason, but it was a heavy burden on both of us. Rob took it so much better than me and was calm and accepting of what had happened, so I tried to feed off his energy. He decided it was time to write his letter of resignation, to let all his customers know when he'd be closing the doors, walking away entirely with no obligation to anyone.

Suddenly, I realised that was exactly why things had unfolded the way they did—Rob had to make the decision to walk away without any ties.

This was bigger than any monetary value that was attached to a sale.

This was his clear path to freedom.

This was his letting go.

We wrote the email together and he pressed the send button. I felt his anxiety as we sat back and waited for the responses. Within minutes, the phone started ringing. We let it go to voicemail for a little while. The news was a shock to a lot of people Rob had worked with for many years, so we felt it was best to give them space to work through their own feelings before Rob had to bear the brunt of their reactions and emotions. It was time to put his own needs first.

It was a day full of processing. Knowing we'd taken the next step by setting a date and committing to the actual closure meant more decisions could be made and plans put in place.

I decided to close my clinic for the next few months in order to put 100% effort into doing what we needed to do together to make this happen. We were all making sacrifices. Rob and I spent long hours at the workshop and onsite, often with Tim and Maddie delivering food to us at night so we could keep working.

We knew in the end it would all be worth it; it just felt like such a massive job.

It was busy, hectic, and Rob was still putting a lot of pressure on himself to go above and beyond. That wasn't going to change in the next three months! It was a huge thing to be walking away from. A lot of people struggled to understand why we would close a successful, profitable company, but we'd both finally reached the point in our lives where neither of us wanted to continue down that path. The value we placed on our lives was so much higher than that. It was time to change our life, and we were the only ones who could do it.

Once we got through that first stage of the process, things started to fall into place quiet smoothly and we realised we'd become more aligned with what was meant to happen. Vehicles and stock were sold, our employees started to get job offers, and then someone offered to purchase the workshop without us even advertising it. It almost seemed too good to be true as all our hard work began to pay off and our dream started to become a reality.

It was a great reminder of how life starts to flow when you let go. Each time we came up against a roadblock it was a sign that it was not the right road to take. Although I knew this in my heart and tried to practice it in my everyday life, I realised how much we'd been trying to *make* things happen instead of *allowing* them to happen. When we were trying to make things happen it felt like we were swimming against the current of the ocean—all we were doing was becoming more and more exhausted, getting nowhere. When we allowed, it felt like we were flowing in the river.

I finally felt like I could start to breathe a little deeper.

We committed to our plan of taking a year off to travel around Australia when it was all over. We'd just go with the flow and see what opportunities arose and where our hearts took us. It gave us a greater purpose to keep moving forward towards our goals. We were at the workshop a high percentage of the time, but when we weren't, we were preparing our car and caravan for our trip. I'm pretty sure the kids didn't believe we were going to go for a whole year. I knew it was going to be really hard for me to be away from them for that long, but I also had no doubt in my mind that it was exactly what we would do.

Reflection Song: I Release Control—Alexa Sunshine Rose

50

Another Year

'Grief never ends, but it changes. It is a passage, not a place to stay. Grief is not a sign of weakness or a lack of faith. It is the price of love.'
Elizabeth I

June 2020

Six years since we lost our beautiful Ella. Another June long weekend had arrived to haunt us. The feeling in my heart as I sat by her graveside was hard to describe.

It was heavy.

Cold.

The middle of winter.

Looking out over the paddock below, I saw the horses moving around slowly. *I know you would love to be here with the horses, Ella.* A little magpie hopped up to her grave and sat on top of the heart-shaped headstone I'd designed, five sunflowers engraved into the side. He looked at me as tears rolled down my cheeks. I wondered what he was thinking or what message he had for me.

I turned to see Ella, in her yellow dress, smiling at me from her photo on the headstone.

Your smile makes me smile. You gave so much to this world, Ella, in such a short space of time, and continue to do so every single day. What an honour it is to be your mum.

Two days ago, I'd felt numb.

Overnight I was very unsettled and nauseous.

On the morning, I woke with a heavy head and heart.

As I made my cup of sweet chai tea, the tears started to fall. I never know what to expect as each year passes. I just feel so, so sad. Broken. There is a part of me inside that will never heal, no matter how much work I do on myself, and that is ok.

This weekend is always one of unpredictable emotions. Every year, I try to allow it all to come. I make no plans. I sit with it, in it, connecting to myself the best way I can.

I often feel like doing something creative at these times. I guess it helps me to go within and find some peace, to get away from the tormenting thoughts that drag me down. I decided to paint a special pot for Ella and plant succulents in it. It felt therapeutic.

Feeling so tired and exhausted, I needed to be still.

What would you look like now? It's coming up to your seventeenth birthday soon. I can only imagine how beautiful you would be with your blue eyes and long blonde hair. What would your dreams be for the future?

These are things I will never know.

Things I was never meant to know.

I miss you Ella.

I love you.

I'd started to have issues with my heart going out of rhythm again, which wasn't surprising, considering the stress I'd been under over the past year. I went back to the heart specialist, who did a number of tests and recommended I go on preventative medication, just in case it happened while we were away travelling. This wasn't something I was at all keen on. Talking with him about the lifestyle change we were about to embark on, knowing in my heart that it would change things on so many levels, I decided to take the script with me just as a precaution and see what happened.

I never got it filled.

Stress can have so many implications on our physical bodies. I've felt it myself and have witnessed it so many times with clients who were committed to reducing their stress levels by changing their lifestyle, which in turn reduced their physical symptoms.

When people get stressed, they often focus on future events and have difficulty living in the present moment. I can relate to that. Stress creates tension in our bodies and minds, making it hard to concentrate. We might also feel unmotivated, uninspired, agitated and fatigued, so while we're usually trying to get things done faster, it often takes us longer because of these symptoms, which in themselves create more stress. It's a vicious cycle.

When I experienced higher levels of stress, I started to bring in more mindfulness activities like:
- Walking each morning in silence before beginning my day.
- Taking time to sit and have my morning cup of tea without rushing.
- Taking short breaks during the day to step outside and breathe deeply for a few minutes.
- Practicing gratitude on a daily basis.
- Eating mindfully and healthily.
- Being kind to myself, even if at times that meant saying no to others.
- Meditating.
- Listening to calming music as I fell asleep.

Each of these little things made a huge difference in helping me to manage my own stress. Feeling blessed to have more free time on the next part of my journey, I would make sure I included more of these things as a priority in my life as I moved into a very different space.

I had a deep knowing that my heart would sort itself out.

Reflection Song: Winter Bear—Coby Grant

51

Preparation

'Whatever makes you uncomfortable is your biggest opportunity for growth.'
Bryant H McGill

The business was closed, everything sold, and we were now taking time to feel into and navigate the next part of our lives.

The sale of the workshop settled. It was such a weird feeling driving away from it all, knowing we never had to go back there, having gratitude for the opportunity we'd created to now be in a position where we could live out our dreams, yet also knowing fully what had been sacrificed for this to be achieved.

We both had mixed emotions. It all felt a little surreal.

During a celebratory lunch at a vineyard, we sat looking at each other with feelings of excitement for what was to come, disbelief of where we were at in our lives and amazement that we'd actually survived not only the last twelve months, but the last fourteen years and had created a pathway for so much opportunity and freedom.

It is so hard to sum up in words all we were feeling that day.

Settling in at home was tricky. We'd planned to leave in about six weeks' time on our big trip around Australia and there was a lot to be done for that to happen, which kept us busy again. I knew it wouldn't be until we got away that we would create the space to process a lot of our emotions and feelings around what our life now looked and felt like, which would be changing every day.

Lots of questions and uncertainties arose for me as we moved closer to our departure date. The trip brought up so many different emotions for us both. It would be an incredible opportunity to have the time and space to be together that we'd been waiting for, for so long. I was really looking forward to that part. Nevertheless, we'd never actually spent that much time at home together in our fourteen years as a couple, let alone in a confined space for an extended period of time. These were some of the things that I trusted would work themselves out organically over time.

I felt anxious and scared, yet excited and grateful. Being connected so deeply to my emotions can be challenging and can often make me feel like I am 'too much' for some people; however, if the tradeoff for that is a life full of deep connections and meaningful relationships, it's 100%worth it. It has taken me many years to be able to recognise all the sensations that my body experiences and acknowledge their existence, importance, meaning and value in my life, even in the moments when it can feel so overwhelming.

This is me.
This is who I am.

Beautifully complicated and full of feelings I don't want to hide.

Vulnerable and not afraid to be seen.

I cannot imagine my life being any different to this—open to feeling the full range of emotions so deeply that I have experienced things on a spectrum I never thought was even possible. This is how I want to live my life.

I have no regrets.

Everything I've had to go through to get to where I am today has given me so many gifts that I would never have had without the pain I've felt and the grief I've had to experience.

I have learnt that when I put more focus and energy into my pain and suffering, I separate myself from the joy life has to offer, so I will continue to focus on bringing joy into my life by creating new experiences and spending my time with those who match this frequency, especially on the days when it does not come so easily.

Learning to live from a space where grief, joy and love can co-exist has been one of my biggest challenges and one of the greatest gifts I have ever received.

I feel so blessed to possess such a strong sense of hope, trust and faith in the Universe. I strongly believe anything is possible and know that with this belief comes so many possibilities, opening me up to endless opportunities in this lifetime.

Preparing for our departure, I had an internal battle going on within my heart around leaving my children, who were now adults. I knew they wanted me to do the trip, and both were excited for us to be having the adventure of a lifetime, but I also knew we'd all miss each other terribly. The longest time I'd ever been away from them was three weeks.

The fact that I had no choice to leave Ella—that choice being taken away from me—and now I was *choosing* to leave my boys, was really tearing at my heart. Yet I knew, deep down, this was something I had to do. I knew there was so much growth awaiting all of us by me going.

Not just for Rob and I, but for Sam, Tim and Maddie as well.

Standing in your truth is sometimes the hardest thing you will ever have to do. For me, it was not just about what I needed to do and be for myself, it was

about the example I was setting for my boys. I wanted to show them that dreams can become reality, that being brave and having hope, even in the presence of fear, is how we can create an extraordinary life of purpose and meaning even after facing devastation and great loss.

We'd talked about this for a long time, and it was now time to put it all into place. The loudest and most impactful action of all is making the commitment, following it through and being impeccable with your own words.

People will watch from a distance, and questions will arise within themselves about their own life.

My wish is that someone:
- Gets inspired in some way.
- Looks at their own life differently.
- Understands the value of the time they have here.
- Feels brave enough to step out of their comfort zone.
- Finds enough courage to make the changes in life they want to make.
- Steps through their fear and comes out the other side braver.
- Stops long enough to feel their own pain to allow it to move through their body.
- Understands themselves a little better.
- Opens their heart.
- Treats themselves more kindly.
- Finds their voice and speaks their truth.
- Becomes more connected and aware of their own behaviours so they may create change and deep connections.

- Puts their own needs first and makes themselves a priority in their life.
- Gets curious about their own stories they've been telling themselves for years that may not be true.
- Takes full responsibility for themselves.
- Finds acceptance in the things they cannot change.
- Hugs their child a little longer and never takes anything for granted.

As Brené Brown puts it, '…resilience is more available to people curious about their own line of thinking and behaving'. I believe this is where my resilience comes from. It has never been an option for me not to explore myself on a deep level. It's not just a curiosity for me—it is a calling and feels like there is actually no other way.

It was time for me to let go and allow everything around me to flow again.

To take a step back and breathe.

To sit in the spaciousness.

To enjoy every moment of every day and embrace the journey ahead—whatever that may be. It felt like I was about to throw a handful of glitter in the air and see where it landed and sparkled.

It was time to surrender.

Because life is too short.

And none of us know how long we've got here.

Reflection Song: Glitter In The Air—Pink

52

Surprise!

'You are worthy of being chosen, fought for, and loved. Remember that.'
Mark Groves

One of my friends organised for us to do something together before I went away. She wouldn't tell me what it was, just to meet her at her house. Feeling exhausted, I'd only said to my sister on the phone that morning that I didn't know if I felt like going anywhere that day. She encouraged me to go, telling me it was probably just what I needed and she was sure I'd have a good time, whatever it was we were doing. She was probably right, so off I went with no idea what was happening.

As I approached her door, I got a glimpse of a centerpiece in the middle of a circle on the floor. Then, as I walked through the doorway, there was my sister, my mum, my two nieces, and some of my most precious friends, all standing with their arms forming an arch, waiting for me to walk through.

I couldn't believe what was happening. These were some of the most important women in my life and they were all together in the same room, at the same time, for me! Tears streamed down my face. Never had I felt so much love. These women were all woven into my tapestry of life to create the person I had become and was becoming. It was so beautifully overwhelming.

As they placed a glorious fresh flower crown on my head, we all sat together in circle. Messages of gratitude were shared as I was held in that space and acknowledged for how much I had given to those around me. I was told it was now my turn to receive.

What a special moment that was. My heart was overflowing, and I felt so humbled to know that my contribution to the world had made a difference to other people's lives in some small way.

> **When women come together to support each other it weaves an invisible net of love that supports us.**
> **Giving us strength when we are weak.**
> **Rejoicing with us in celebration when we are strong.**

This was the whole reason I continued to offer spaces for women to come together. There is a sacred connection that takes place within a circle of women that can only be felt deep within the hearts of those present. To be honoured in that way is something I'm not sure I'll ever be able to portray in words alone.

We sang, we danced, we laughed, cried, created, ate, and drank. We celebrated life.

I feel forever blessed to have all these incredible women in my life, along with all the special women who couldn't be there.

Allowing myself to sit in the magic of the day and feel all the emotions I'd never experienced at that level before,

Part 2 – Surprise!

I realised how truly blessed my life was and saw my own worthiness in the reflection of those who surrounded me.

We are all mirrors for each other.

Reflection Song: Worthy—India Arie

53

The Next Part of the Journey

*'Dare to live the life you have dreamed
for yourself. Go forward and make your
dreams come true.'*
Ralph Waldo Emerson

At 10 pm on a Thursday night, August 7, 2020, we hugged our children goodbye and got in our car. With our caravan packed and hooked on, we drove off into the darkness.

The feeling was surreal.

We'd made some big decisions over the last year, taken massive steps and made huge sacrifices to get to this moment, and here it was. As we drove up the highway, we turned to each other at the same time with a look of excitement, trepidation and disbelief.

We'd just driven away from everything we knew.

We laughed out loud and high-fived each other.

Our plan was to travel around Australia for the next year, but all we knew right then was that our first goal was to get over the Queensland border within the next twenty-four hours before it closed.

We didn't know what this part of our life journey would bring, but one thing we did know was that we were living from a place inside our hearts that had been calling us home now for far too long.

It was time for us both to go within.

To find ourselves a little more.
To meet new people and experience places we'd never been.
To step out of our comfort zones in order to grow.
To live.

I believe that no matter how long we live for, when it's our time to leave this world, we have served our purpose here—whether this is when we are ten years old or one hundred years old. This may not always be able to be immediately seen or felt by those who are sadly left behind to process their pain and loss, but as we start to heal from the inside out and create space to feel and receive, we will have the opportunity to see the incredible gifts that may not have been possible to share with our loved ones while we were together on this earth.

Grief is one of the most difficult experiences and processes we will all have to go through. We cannot escape it.

When grief becomes a gift we are able to have a deep appreciation of the preciousness of life and the depth of love that we are all capable of.

Let go, open your heart, step into life, and keep shining brightly.

You are a gift to this world.

≈

Reflection Song: Home—Phillip Phillips

It's Time
It's time to let the walls down,
Be honest and be true,
Step into unknown places
Listen carefully, follow through.

This is a new beginning,
Surrendering, letting go,
The future path now cleared,
For new energy to flow.

Challenges will still come,
Emotions may be raw,
Some hiding in the smallest cracks,
Just waiting for space to be explored.

Stepping bravely into my future,
That only I can create,
Guided by my heart's yearning,
Making the choices I need to make.

I've survived the deepest heartache,
The darkest of dark days,
Learning so many lessons,
Continually growing along the way.

Whatever is in front of me,
I am open to receive,
Learning why I came here,
Remembering to believe.

Knowing there is always more,
Healing from the Inside Out,
Finding gifts in deep, dark places,
Discovering what I am all about.

                                            Kim Cameron

Our Life with Ella

Kim, Ella, Rob, Tim & Sam. Holidaying in Fiji.

Our beautiful flower girl. Kim & Rob's Wedding Day. January 2013.

Ella & Sam. Christmas 2013.

Ella's last school photo.

Paddleboarding. January 2014.

Kim's 40th fancy dress party; her last birthday with Ella.

Ella at the War Memorial in Canberra. April 2014 School Camp.

Kim & Rob. Ella's Memorial Walk. September 2015.

Sam, Kim & Tim. Ella's Ball. 2016.

Sam, Rob, Kim & Tim. The Day we departed on our trip around Australia. August 2020.

ELLA
6TH JUNE 2014

YOU WILL ALWAYS BE OUR SUNSHINE.

Important Things I've Learnt on This Journey

'We must be willing to let go of the life we've planned, so as to have the life that is waiting for us.'
Joseph Campbell

Finding acceptance in the things I cannot change has been key to being able to move gently from the darkness into the light.

Loving myself enough to invest time, money and energy into my healing and growth is a non-negotiable priority.

∞

Taking time out with myself in silence is where I am able to connect deeply to my own intuition and trust it fully.

Making conscious choices and decisions about how I want to live my life and show up in the world allows me to step into my power and make choices that support its creation.

Important Things I've Learnt on This Journey

Being present and deeply listening means I can hold space for others.

Becoming comfortable with other people not understanding my journey means I never have to waste time worrying about what they think—because it is none of my business.

Believing that I am only a small part of an entire universe helps me to put things into perspective and let go of the things that don't matter and are not worth my time and energy.

Valuing each moment I am given to walk upon this earth gives me a passion and determination to find my purpose while I am here.

Feeling gratitude and never taking anything for granted results in a deep appreciation for life.

Seeking out help when my emotions feel too heavy and overwhelming means I am taking responsibility for myself.

Real healing is a deconditioning process. It always starts with loving yourself first.

∞

Understanding that my greatest transformations happen when I move through my own anxiety and fears.

∞

Listening to my body and its wisdom through messages of pain is one of my greatest teachers.

∞

Investing time into relationships that are important to me deepens the connection.

∞

Knowing I get to choose how I respond in each moment of my life is empowering.

∞

Being aware that when my walls are up and I am trying to protect myself from potential pain, I am also preventing the flow of love coming through.

∞

Being brave enough to try is better than not trying at all.

∞

Important Things I've Learnt on
This Journey

The less attached I am the more peace I feel.

Nature is the best place to go when I want to calm my mind, connect to myself, and remember what I already know in my heart.

Grief and joy can co-exist, side by side.

Deep listening results in deep understanding.

The depth of my grief is a reflection of the deep love I have for Ella, and that is a beautiful gift.

An Invitation for Reflection and Deeper Connection

Journal Questions & Processes

Suggestion

Download your *free* Inside Out - Reflection and Connection Journal, which contains all these questions and more, at www.kimcameronholistictherapies.com.au.

Or you may choose to grab your own notebook and work through the questions and exercises at your own pace as you step within yourself to create deeper connection.

You can start at the beginning and move down the list of questions slowly over time, or you may find there are specific questions that call you. Be aware that the questions we resist the most are often the ones we need to look at the deepest.

Take your time, be gentle and kind. Get curious about yourself.

EXPLORE   LISTEN   FEEL   TRUST

If you found out you were going to lose someone you loved dearly, long before you thought you would, what would be the most important things for you to do?

∞

Have you ever had to say goodbye to someone after they passed away and felt like you needed more time to process and express how you felt?
- Is there any way you would like to do this differently next time?

∞

Have you ever felt uncomfortable speaking with someone who has lost a loved one, wondering what the 'right' thing to say is?
- How did you feel in their presence?
- Having this self-awareness creates a beautiful opportunity to get curious about why it might be this way for you.

∞

How do you honour and look after yourself when you are grieving?
- Remembering that grief is not just experienced when we lose people we love.

∞

Have you ever lost someone and noticed how the men and women in your life grieve differently?
- Have you ever found yourself judging anyone based on these differences and your own beliefs?

∞

How do you grieve? Do you feel you are more of an instrumental or intuitive griever?
- What is useful for you during these times? This is important to know, so you can recognise the tools that you already have to draw on.

∞

Is there anyone in your life you've been meaning to connect with in some way, but have not made it a priority to do so?
- Think about what you'd like to say to them, or do with them, and make it happen—because tomorrow is never guaranteed.

∞

What would you do today if you knew you would not be here tomorrow?

∞

Who are the people in your life that you know would be there for you if you needed them, in a heartbeat, for months and years after a tragedy, no questions asked?
- Do you value the connection you have with them?
- How could you continue to nurture these connections?

∞

How do you feel within yourself when people around you are experiencing emotional pain?
- Do you ever feel like you want to take their pain away?
- Is it hard for you to sit with someone in silence, just holding their hand and being fully present, without feeling there is something you have to do or fix?

∞

Has anything significant happened to you in your life, and when you look back in hindsight, you realise there were so many signs leading up to the event that you never noticed at the time, but seem so obvious now?

- What were they and what did they mean to you once you connected with them?

∞

Have you ever had a feeling of deep knowing in your gut and followed your own intuition, regardless of other people's opinions?
- Do you remember the energy of this and what it felt like?
- What was the outcome of trusting your own intuition?

∞

Have you ever had a spiritual experience that you have questioned or felt uncertain about sharing in case others didn't believe you?
- What was your experience like for you?
- Allow yourself to relive it. Become aware of the feelings that are remembered when you step back into this space, knowing no-one can ever take that moment away from you.

∞

How do you react or respond when you feel fear or anxiety?
- What physical sensations do you feel in your body and where?
- How do you move through these feelings?

What resources help you navigate through these times—internally and externally?

∞

Is it easier for you to give or receive?
- What part of giving or receiving is challenging for you?

∞

Can you recognise a cycle or pattern you may have adopted that has been passed down through past generations within your own family?
- If this is a pattern you would like to step out of, what steps could you start to take to commence this transition for yourself?

∞

What would you do if you knew you could not fail?

∞

Have you ever held onto wanting a specific outcome so tightly that it was difficult to let go of it when it didn't arrive the way you expected?

Bring it to your awareness now:
- What if you had no expectations to begin with? How might this have felt different?

∞

Are you someone who gives a lot of yourself to others?
- Does this have any negative impact on you emotionally, physically, mentally or spiritually?
- How do you feel when you have given too much of yourself?
- What is one thing you could do to start to change this pattern?
- What needs of yours are being met by others when you put their needs in front of your own? (This can be a tricky question, but an extremely important one—read it again.)

∞

What holds you back, or what do you see as an obstacle for not taking time out for yourself?
- Be consciously aware of not blaming others.
- This is an opportunity to take full responsibility for the choices you are making for yourself in this lifetime.

Do you feel worthy enough to put yourself first?
- Why?
- Why not?

Have you ever had a moment in your life where you've allowed yourself to fully let go of all fear and resistance, totally surrender, and trust the flow of life?
- If you have—what did this feel like for you?
- If you haven't—what stops you?

Can you recognise a wound you might be carrying that feels heavy, calling for your attention? Be honest with yourself and write it down. Name it:
- It could be something that triggers you, causing an emotional response or reaction.
- It could be contributing to physical pain in your body.
- It could be grief or trauma you have never given time and space to process.
- Acknowledge how long you have been carrying this wound around.

Become aware of any avoidance towards acknowledging this wound:

- How do you react to this each time it is brought to your attention?
- How does your body feel?
- Do you feel this wound impacts your life and how you show up in the world?
- Does it have an impact on those around you?
- What support do you need to begin healing this part of you to improve the quality of your life?

Do you know what your values are?
- If you don't, get curious about what they might be (refer to the online journal for suggestions on how to do this).
- If you do, ask yourself if you're living your life in alignment with these.
- If not, is there something you need to do so that they align, for you to show up as a more authentic version of yourself in the world.

Is your heart open, ready to give and receive love?
- Do you ever feel like you are blocking people from fully connecting with you?
- Acknowledge how you do this and why you feel this might happen.
- Is there something you are holding onto that you need to let go of that is creating a blockage?
- What changes could you make personally to allow love to flow freely in and out of your life?

∞

Is there someone in your life you need to forgive to set yourself free?
- Forgiveness is not about condoning any bad behaviour of others; it is about releasing the hold it has on you, meaning you no longer allow someone else to impact your emotions.
- Once forgiveness has taken place there is no-one to blame.

∞

How does your body feel when things are out of balance for you?
- What are some of the behaviours that present themselves when you are feeling this way?
- What are some of the tools you currently use to rebalance yourself?
- Is there something you would like to bring more of into your life to feel more balance?

∞

Are you aware of any addictive behaviours or habits that you have, or have had, in your life that you've used as a distraction to numb your own pain?
- What would the benefits be for you to work towards replacing these behaviours with more nurturing ones, and what might these look like?
- What support would you need to begin to make these changes?

Is there something you really want to do in life that brings up feelings of anxiousness or uncertainty?
- What is it? Write it down in huge letters so you can see it every day.
- Ask yourself—what is the worst thing that could happen, and what could be the possible benefits for you if you stepped out of your comfort zone towards this dream?
- Remember that change is always on the other side of fear.

Have you ever set high expectations for yourself and been disappointed when you could not achieve them?
- What are your feelings around lowering your expectations and letting go of the 'pushing' energy that may be behind them?
- What difference do you think this would make to how your body feels when you release this pressure you have been placing on yourself?

Emotions are our messengers. When emotions arise for you, do you stop and listen to what they are trying to tell you with openness, interest and curiosity?
- Or do you shut them down quickly, pushing them back into your body until they rise again at another time, trying desperately to get your attention?

- Try to become aware of your body's response or reaction to your emotions when they present themselves and give them space to be felt.

Have you ever felt like you needed to rest, but continued pushing yourself so you didn't disappoint others?
- How did this feel?
- Is this a pattern in your life that you recognise?
- Has it been passed down through generations within your family?
- If this is a pattern you resonate with, how could you start to change it?
- Breaking the cycle by changing the pattern creates powerful transformation.

When was the last time you fully surrendered and allowed yourself to give in to rest completely?

What does family mean to you?
- What does it look like? (Remember family is not always your blood relatives.)
- How do you feel when you are with these people?

Think of an important relationship in your life. Take some time to reflect on the connection you have with this person:
- Do you feel it may benefit from some extra energy and attention?

- What could you do to create a deeper connection with this person to have more open and honest conversations?
- Energy flows where attention goes.

Are there any other areas of your life where you feel you are missing connection?
- If these spaces feel empty, what are some ways you might be able to invite more connection in?

Have you ever lost someone and felt like you would like to honour that person in some way?
- It may be a creative project for yourself to remember them, a donation you'd like to make to a charity or creating a space in your home—like an altar or garden.

It's never too late.
- Take some time to feel into this and put into action whatever feels good for your heart and soul.

If you have lost someone you love, do you notice how things change as time goes on?
- What has changed for you over time?
- Is there something you would like to do differently as part of your grief journey that you have not done in the past to remember your loved one?

∞

What do you do to create memories with the people you love?

∞

Write a list of all the things that bring you joy and happiness in your life.
- Include all the little things that make you smile that you might take for granted.

∞

If you feel you need additional support to work through these reflections and questions, please reach out. I offer personal online Holistic Therapy Sessions, Connection Circles, Group Workshops and Retreats that can assist in deep reflective processing to create stronger connection with self.

I hope you have found something within my writing, through my shared life experiences, that has woven a connective thread of love into your own heart. May you continue to be curious and compassionate with yourself throughout your own journey, connecting deeply from the "Inside Out".

Healing starts with loving yourself, so always make this your starting point.

I would love to hear from you about your experience of reading *Inside Out*, so please feel free to connect with me via my website, email or social media.

Song List

Scan the QR Code below to access the playlist on Spotify.

https://playlist.sptfy.com/insideout-kimcameron

Hand to Hold—JJ Heller
A Mother's Prayer—Céline Dion
Girl—SYML
Life—Sleeping At Last
Fix You—Coldplay
I Want You Here—Plumb
Jealous of the Angels—Donna Taggart
Unconditionally—Katy Perry
The Next Right Thing—Kristen Bell
Graves—Aisha Badru
The Voice Within—Christina Aguilera
I Will Carry You—Selah
Satellite—Ben Abraham
Clouds—Before You Exit
The Last Day on Earth—Kate Miller-Heidke
Trust—Alexia Chellun

Song List

Mad World—Michael Andrews, Gary Jules
A Sky Full of Stars—Coldplay
One Day at a Time—Jeremy Voltz
Prisoners & Guards—Aisha Badru
Like a Lake—Sara Groves
Big Love, Small Moments—JJ Heller
Your Love Walks With Me—Claire Bowditch
The Art of Letting Go—Fia
Ocean—Michael Benjamin
Just Fine (Alternate Version)—Desirée Dawson
I Am—Satsang
Break On Me—Keith Urban
Forgive—Trevor Hall, Luka Lesson
Rise Up—Andra Day
Count on Me—Joy Oladokun
I Chose You Mama—Sarah Humphreys with Loren Kate
Stand By You—Rachel Platten
In Dreams—Jai-Jagdeesh
We Can do Hard Things—Tish Melton
Look For The Good—Jason Mraz
Connection—OneRepublic
Who You Are—Jessie J
Your Best (feat. Lennon & Maisy)—Nashville Cast
Hold My Hand—Nessie Gomes
Sound of Surviving—Nichole Nordeman
Be Slow—Harrison Storm
A Hundred Thousand Angels—Bliss
Carry You—Missy Higgins
Never Giving Up—Fearless Soul
Brave—Sara Bareilles
A Reminder (Remix)—Trevor Hall
Rooted—Aisha Badru

I Release Control—Alexa Sunshine Rose
Winter Bear—Coby Grant
Glitter In The Air—Pink
Worthy—India Arie
Home—Phillip Phillips

Poems by Kim Cameron

I Was
Who Are We
Distance
Being Brave
Accepting Sunshine
Soul Connection
Five Minutes More
Then There Is This
It's Time

Organisations for Support in Australia

Red Nose Australia
https://rednose.org.au/
Grief and Loss Support Line – 24/7: 1300 308 307

Bereavement support free of charge to any person affected by the sudden and unexpected death of a baby or child during pregnancy, birth, infancy or childhood.

Grief Line
https://griefline.org.au/
1300 845 735

Provides free and confidential counselling and support to people experiencing grief and loss across Australia, inclusive of remote, regional, rural and metropolitan regions.

Lifeline
https://www.lifeline.org.au/
Crisis Support – 24/7: 131114

Lifeline provides compassionate support for people in crisis. No judgement. No conditions. No agenda. Just a human connection to help people get through their darkest moments.

Beyond Blue
https://www.beyondblue.org.au/
Brief Counselling – 24/7: 1300 224 636 – Beyond Blue Support Service is available for brief counselling to listen and help you find the extra mental health help you need.

About the Author

Kim is a loving mum of three, whose courage and determination to process her own grief after the tragic loss of her only daughter, Ella, guided her to become a Holistic Therapist and Women's Retreat Facilitator.

Holding qualifications in Mind Body Medicine, Kinesiology, Holistic Counselling, Leadership and Facilitation, Kim creates safe spaces for people to process suppressed emotions, allowing opportunity for energy to flow and deep connection to self.

With a knowing in her heart, Kim saw that change was always on the other side of fear. Committed to her own healing, peeling back the layers of trauma and pain, she found a place of peace and acceptance, where grief and joy could co-exist alongside each other.

A journey she shares through her book "Inside Out".

Her mission is to encourage and promote open, vulnerable discussions around grief and loss, emphasising the importance of feeling all emotions in their fullness that present themselves through the grieving process.

Kim is an authentic, honest, caring soul who has developed a deep connection with her body and mind along with an unwavering sense of trust in her own intuition.

Grateful for each day she wakes up and is given the opportunity to experience life on this earth, she continues to find the gifts within her own grief.

For more information visit:
www.kimcameronholistictherapies.com.au

www.ingramcontent.com/pod-product-compliance
Lightning Source LLC
Chambersburg PA
CBHW061254230426
43665CB00027B/2933